PRAISE FOR
A HEALING SPACE

"Matt Licata pinpoints a space within us where healing, awakening, and a vibrant reckoning of who we actually are can be realized. The wisdom hidden deep within our darkest experiences comes not from turning away from these, but by directly tending to them with gentleness, love, and compassion. This book depicts a way of genuine freedom."

SHARON SALZBERG,
author of *Lovingkindness* and *Real Happiness*

"Matt Licata's *A Healing Space* is a wise, compassionate, and helpful book. While healing is a mystery, we all have to consider, 'What is life asking of me, and how can I bring my mature self to the task?' This book is an accessible, kind, insightful, and useful guide to assist any reader in this good work."

JAMES HOLLIS, PhD,
Jungian analyst and author of *Living Between Worlds*

"Matt Licata's book is a true companion for the journey of being here in Earth school. It's as if he takes you by the hand and heart and gentles the way into the descent of the shadow and the ascent into the light and wholeness of true healing. He has a beautiful, firm, loving grasp of the subtleties and difficulties, the joys, and the ultimate wonders of being human."

GENEEN ROTH,
author of #1 *New York Times* bestseller *Women Food and God* and *This Messy Magnificent Life*

"Tender, profound, and deeply useful, this book is gem. Remarkably, Matt Licata weaves together self-compassion, depth psychology, and radical acceptance into a beautiful, passionate, soaring exploration of all that it means to be human."

RICK HANSON, PhD,
New York Times bestselling author of *Neurodharma*

"A *Healing Space* is a beautiful, insightful, and moving contemplation of the journey of healing we all undertake as human beings. It illuminates how self-compassion—holding our own pain with love—transforms our experience in a profound way so that we can learn the lessons life offers us moment by moment."

KRISTIN NEFF, PhD,
associate professor at the University of Texas
and author of *Self-Compassion*

"A goldmine of wisdom for difficult times, A *Healing Space* offers a profound understanding of the healing process and a deep compassion for those who travel there. Here lies a weaving of depth psychology and alchemy, with a fresh view of spiritual truths and fallacies. It shows us that true healing begins only when we stop looking for the quick fixes and fully embrace our wounds. Rich and soulful, it is a must-read for anyone on their healing journey, and for all practitioners who guide them. This book is the kind of therapist we all wish we could find."

ANODEA JUDITH, PhD,
founder and director of Sacred Centers and
author of *Eastern Body, Western Mind*
and *Charge and the Energy Body*

"This inspiring book invites us to trust the intelligence of whatever is unfolding in our lives, especially when it hurts, and to meet it in a deeply compassionate way. Matt Licata is a cartographer of the human heart. He knows the ineffable space where healing occurs and offers us a map for getting there, right up to the threshold. The rest is alchemy. We have been waiting a long time for a book like this."

CHRISTOPHER GERMER, PhD,
clinical psychologist and lecturer at Harvard Medical
School, author of *The Mindful Path to Self-Compassion*, and
co-developer of the Mindful Self-Compassion program

"Matt Licata's book is a thoughtful and gentle approach to how we might heal ourselves and others. This book leads us on a practical and compassionate healing path without the complexities of much theory. I heartily recommend it to anyone interested in the mysteries of the healing journey."

LIONEL CORBETT, MD,
psychiatrist, Jungian analyst, professor of
depth psychology at Pacifica Graduate Institute,
and author of *The Sacred Cauldron*

"In *A Healing Space*, Matt Licata skillfully and gently introduces the reader into some of the most important and least-discussed work in personal spiritual development—the play of the unconscious and unilluminated parts of self. I applaud him for bringing this to all of us and highly recommend this book for anyone interested in personal healing. This is the 'secret' recipe for a transformational journey that must be taken yet requires guidance to achieve. I am thrilled to see Dr. Licata taking the leap to sharing this work with anyone who has the courage to engage it."

ANN MARIE CHIASSON, MD,
director of the Fellowship in Integrative Medicine, associate
professor of clinical medicine at the University of Arizona Andrew
Weil Center for Integrative Medicine, and author of *Energy Healing*
and *Self-Healing with Energy Medicine* (with Dr. Andrew Weil)

"*A Healing Space* is a brilliant weave of Jungian and Eastern contemplative wisdom. In this powerful new offering, Matt Licata guides us to a place of sacred refuge, where we can meet even our greatest moments of confusion and suffering with compassion and grace."

TARA BRACH, PhD,
author of *Radical Compassion*

"*A Healing Space* invites us to explore and endeavor the alchemist's way of facing the tough stuff that haunts us. Matt Licata, skilled psychotherapist and spirit-beacon, offers respite for the troubled soul. Along the way, he prepares us with the exercises necessary to face the wounded psyche, question its purpose in our lives, and go through the middle of it in order to free the best parts of ourselves. Healing is a tricky thing, and Matt is just the one to guide us through the psychic fog. He writes with the vulnerability of a poet and the insight of a master alchemist to help us shape what remains a recurrent struggle into a form we can face, question, and—with practice—balance and embrace."

STAN TATKIN, PSYD, MFT,
developer of the Psychobiological Approach to Couples Therapy
(PACT) and author of *We Do* and *Wired for Love*

"If you are looking for a book to be a companion to you during this extraordinary time, it's this one. *A Healing Space* is a robust guidebook into the inner territory of yourself, assisting you in the exploration of deep and rich personal and life questions that lead, always, to wondrous realizations and growth. What a treasure to find in these times of great change."

CAROLINE MYSS,
author of *Anatomy of the Spirit* and *Intimate Conversations with the Divine*

"Weaving the wisdom of reflective practices, the insights of Carl Jung and the alchemists, and the relational truths of attachment research and psychotherapy practice, Matt Licata offers us a beautiful tapestry of truths to transform trauma into healing and strength. Adversity can constrain us, but with this wonderful book we can find the perspectives and courage to embrace the reality of life's innate uncertainty to guide us on a journey of growth and discovery—moving from post-traumatic imprisonment to liberation."

DANIEL J. SIEGEL, MD,
clinical professor at UCLA School of Medicine,
director of the Mindsight Institute,
and author of *Aware* and *Mindsight*

"Matt Licata has become an important and eloquent voice inviting us to go to, rather than avoid, what seem like unbearable emotions buried in our dark depths. From his Jungian perspective, he provides needed reassurance that doing so will achieve alchemical transformations in which what we thought were inner toxins turn out to be our gold. He also offers a cogent critique of the spiritual bypassing and ego bashing that is rampant within many spiritualities."

RICHARD C. SCHWARTZ, PhD,
developer of the Internal Family Systems (IFS) model,
adjunct faculty of the Department of Psychiatry
at Harvard Medical School, and author of
more than fifty articles and books

"This is a book about love. The kind of love that embraces all parts of ourselves and others with generosity, tenderness, and strength. Matt is clear that this quality of receptivity does not develop easily or quickly. It is not a decision of the mind so much as an opening of the heart, so no part of us is abandoned in the healing process. Challenging our society's tendency to fix, leave, or devalue states considered negative, he extends welcome to darkness, death, confusion, doubt, and all their companions as instructive friends in their own right, not just as the prelude to light and rebirth. He illuminates the pathway to Rumi's 'Guest House,' where our shame and malice are equally welcome and held in healing compassion. In truth, each of us yearns for sanctuary for these parts, and Matt is a wise and empathic companion along this healing path."

BONNIE BADENOCH, PhD,
author of *The Heart of Trauma* and *Being a Brain-Wise Therapist*

"In *A Healing Space*, Matt Licata serves as a compassionate and insightful guide to the transformative task we all must face: how to forge our pain and sorrow into remedies of Spirit that can illuminate our way. With the soft clarity of a magnifying glass, Matt brings into view the many things that inhabit our nature, though they are seldom easily seen. Stay in conversation with this book and you will be a better friend to yourself, those you travel with, and to life itself."

MARK NEPO,
author of *The Book of Soul* and *Drinking from the River of Light*

"*A Healing Space* is a beautifully written and masterful handbook, both profound and practical, that reveals the road we all must travel to navigate the inevitable challenges that life brings us throughout our lives, to help us fulfill our potential as fully alive and authentic human beings. I cannot think of a better book to be reading in this moment, or at any time along your journey through life. A must-read!"

RICHARD MILLER, PhD,
author of *The iRest Program for Healing PTSD*,
iRest Meditation, and *Yoga Nidra*

"A deep-diving, beautifully nuanced exploration of cultivating intimacy with all that we are, including whatever in us we are inclined to reject or shun. Matt's presentation of all this is not only lucidly articulated, but always caring, no matter how edgy the terrain. Highly recommended!"

ROBERT AUGUSTUS MASTERS, PhD,
author of *Spiritual Bypassing, Emotional Intimacy*,
and *Bringing Your Shadow Out of the Dark*

"*A Healing Space* invites us to discover and create a way of being with our challenging experience that is intimate, loving, and deeply transformative—in Jungian terms, *alchemical*. Drawing from his years as a depth psychotherapist and contemplative practitioner, Matt Licata brings a mature and nuanced understanding to subtle psychospiritual issues and encourages readers to trust their own unique unfolding. Eloquent and inspiring."

JOHN J. PRENDERGAST, PhD,
author of *The Deep Heart* and *In Touch*, retired adjunct
professor of psychology, teacher, and psychotherapist

"Matt Licata offers guidance, support, and above all, companionship for the most important journey of all: coming back to yourself. He offers a crucially important lesson—that personal healing and spiritual awakening are not the self-abandonment that some teachings may suggest, but rather a process of becoming more fully alive. He writes clearly and passionately, straight from his heart to yours."

JUDITH BLACKSTONE, PhD,
founder of the Realization Process and
author of *Trauma and the Unbound Body*

"As we enter an era of radical uncertainty, it is vital that we find the inner tools, both psychological and spiritual, to guide and support us. Rather than retreating into fear and isolation, we need to embrace the difficulties, the insecurity that life is bringing us. Grounded in the ancient tradition of alchemy, Matt Licata gives us access to a space for real healing and transformation, showing us how to grow through the darkness and discover the true gold of our inner self. We come to experience how we are inwardly held, enabling us to open to a new world and step into unfamiliar experiences. *A Healing Space* offers essential wisdom to help us to live with compassion and kindness to ourselves and others, to discover how our wounds and grief are pathways to a deeper love."

LLEWELLYN VAUGHAN-LEE, PhD,
Sufi teacher and author of *Love is a Fire*

"This is a book you will treasure for a lifetime. It's more than a book, really. It's a compassionate, nonjudgmental, and wise companion that gently helps you explore what it means to be deeply, courageously, and honestly human."

MARTIN L. ROSSMAN, MD,
clinical instructor at the University of California
Medical Center, San Francisco, and author of
The Worry Solution and *Fighting Cancer from Within*

"*A Healing Space* elegantly weaves together contemporary approaches in neuroscience and depth psychology with the ancient wisdom of the contemplative traditions, providing a modern, integrated path of deep transformation that fills in what might be missing in each separately. Matt Licata emphasizes radical befriending that reorients our inner critic in a kind way. This book lands in the heart and is ultimately about the power of love to heal trauma and attachment injuries. We need this fresh vision and perspective. Matt definitely delivers."

DIANE POOLE HELLER, PhD,
founder of Dynamic Attachment Re-Patterning Experience and author of
The Power of Attachment and *Crash Course*

"In this well-written book, Matt Licata challenges us to remember our disavowed parts, our painful emotions and traumas, and to treat each as if it were a lost friend needing our attention. In this way, though often difficult, we can arrive at a state of wholeness, embrace in a gentle, loving way those previously unwanted and unsupported aspects of ourselves, and become the person we were meant to be. Matt supports this process with great attention and compelling narrative and offers us a hand up in this challenging but essential task."

JEFFREY RAFF, PhD,
Jungian analyst and author of several books, including
Jung and the Alchemical Imagination and *The Practice of Ally Work*

"In the opening pages of *A Healing Space*, Matt Licata draws us into a meditative intimacy with the gift and miracle of our bodies, minds, and hearts. He keeps us there, offering trustworthy guidance in the gentle art of touching the hurting places within ourselves and others with tender-hearted clarity and love."

JAMES FINLEY, PhD,
clinical psychologist, former monk, spiritual directee of
Thomas Merton, and author of *Merton's Palace of Nowhere*

"*A Healing Space* is a compelling invitation to embark on a bold personal journey—to dive deeply, consciously, into the pain of an unlived life. To radically trust in the process of intuitive inquiry. To be with and befriend, claim, and cherish the deepest, most intimate, sometimes disdained parts of ourselves. To listen to the wisdom and intelligence of their messages. To be held in that process in an inner, felt sense of sacred safety and loving presence. To become fully known and to reemerge in a radically new apprehension of the entirety of one's self, fully alive, fully participating in life's vast mysteries and possibilities, in difficult times, in all times. Matt Licata is more than a respected authority and trustworthy guide; he is a compassionate companion on this journey, providing the metaphors and markers needed to navigate the 'green goo' of the chrysalis as the humble caterpillar morphs into the beauty and freedom of the butterfly. He illuminates for the reader the nuanced complexities of this paradoxical dance of being and becoming, fully alive, already healed."

LINDA GRAHAM, MFT,
psychotherapist and author of *Resilience*

"Happiness is indeed a unique individual journey. *A Healing Space* provides a magnificent broad overview and personal spiritual path to inner peace during these current challenges."

C. NORMAN SHEALY, MD, PhD,
founding president of the American Holistic Medical Association

"Despite our desire to live in the moment, most of us live in the past: rehearsing old dramas and applying old solutions to new challenges. In *A Healing Space*, Matt Licata offers us away out of the past and into the present. Not an easy way, but an authentic one. This book is not meant to be a page turner, but a life saver. Use it wisely."

RABBI RAMI SHAPIRO,
author of *Holy Rascals*

"Matt Licata has written the perfect book for these unprecedented times, exploring the overlapping fields of psychological and emotional development."

LAMA TSULTRIM ALLIONE,
Buddhist teacher and author of *Wisdom Rising*

"*A Healing Space* opens up an engaged pathway into the alchemical tradition of depth psychology, where Matt Licata offers powerful and responsible ways to work on oneself. As opposed to popular volumes that feature catchphrases and escapist esoteric fantasies, *A Healing Space* does not reduce the human journey to simplistic steps, but encourages us 'to get messy with the stuff of life' and to have the courage and wherewithal to bear the unbearable. Reminding us that 'emotion is not pathology' and that freedom is found in the embrace of all parts of one's being, this work supports and illumines the journey of conscious awareness."

RICK JAROW, PhD,
associate professor of religious studies at
Vassar College and author of *Creating the Work You Love*,
Alchemy of Abundance, and *The Ultimate Anti-Career Guide*

"You need this book! We all need this book! Though written just before the pandemic hit, this book is a healing balm for the mind, body, and soul as we deal with external and mind-born stressors impacting us right now. Dr. Licata offers his compassionate wisdom, informed by clinical experience and his study of Buddhist traditions and depth psychology, for all of us to benefit from."

LAWRENCE EDWARDS, PhD,
faculty of New York Medical College,
author of *The Soul's Journey* and *Awakening Kundalini*

"In stark contrast to the pressures posed by our always-feel-good culture, *A Healing Space* offers a timely and welcomed invitation to venture deep, to embrace our fragility and wounding, and to access the tenderness we seek to become more fully human. Matt Licata draws on his unique blend of psychotherapy, meditative practice, and poetic imagination to help us transform the immediacy of our own awareness into a life-affirming crucible of unflinching presence and radical acceptance for all that we are and can be. Anyone with the courage to encounter their humanity in all its glory and failings will benefit from the medicinal balm that even a few pages can offer in our time of need."

MILES NEALE, PsyD,
Buddhist psychotherapist, author of *Gradual Awakening*,
and founder of the Contemplative Studies Program

"Because your journey through life, like everyone's journey, is a unique story that has never before been told and will never be told again, no guidebook really fits the territory. Matt Licata's beautifully crafted treatise is about as close as I've seen! From his premise that 'you are not a project to be solved, but a mystery coming into form,' he invites and shows you how to 'open to the unexpected wisdom, creativity, and beauty in your immediate experience.'"

DAVID FEINSTEIN, PhD,
coauthor of *The Energies of Love* and *Energy Medicine*

"Matt Licata's new offering, *A Healing Space*, feels like a love letter to my wild heart—a gift of being witnessed through his poetic and potent words. After spending decades in the realm of dharma teachings that often look through the lens of transcendence, that recommend we overcome being human, this book offers a great exhale. It pierces the veneer and embraces the kaleidoscope that is our messy, raw, vulnerable, and tender being as we attempt to live with more awareness and mend old stories and wounds. It's healing by embracing all the parts. His blend of psychology, spiritual understanding, and lyrical conversations about the whole of life's unfolding makes me feel at home in the whole of my being."

JANET STONE,
yoga teacher and founder of the Stone Yoga School

A HEALING SPACE

ALSO BY MATT LICATA

The Path Is Everywhere:
Uncovering the Jewels Hidden Within You

A
HEALING
SPACE

Befriending Ourselves in Difficult Times

MATT LICATA, PhD

BOULDER, COLORADO

Sounds True
Boulder, CO 80306

This book is not intended as a substitute for the medical recommendations of physicians, mental health professionals, or other health-care providers. Rather, it is intended
to offer information to help the reader cooperate with physicians, mental health professionals, and health-care providers in a mutual quest for optimal well-being. We
advise readers to carefully review and understand the ideas presented and to seek the
advice of a qualified professional before attempting to use them.

Published 2020

Cover design by Lisa Kerans
Book design by Maureen Forys, Happenstance Type-O-Rama

Printed in the United States of America

Library of Congress Cataloging-in-Publication Data
Names: Licata, Matt, author.
Title: A healing space : befriending ourselves in difficult times / by Matt
   Licata, PhD.
Description: Boulder, CO : Sounds True, 2020. | Includes bibliographical
   references.
Identifiers: LCCN 2020007698 (print) | LCCN 2020007699 (ebook) | ISBN
   9781683643739 (paperback) | ISBN 9781683644255 (ebook)
Subjects: LCSH: Self-actualization (Psychology) | Mindfulness (Psychology)
   | Self-acceptance.
Classification: LCC BF637.S4 L48955 2020 (print) | LCC BF637.S4 (ebook) |
   DDC 158.1—dc23
LC record available at https://lccn.loc.gov/2020007698
LC ebook record available at https://lccn.loc.gov/2020007699

10 9 8 7 6 5 4 3 2

CONTENTS

FOREWORD

by Mirabai Starr

I DON'T KNOW ABOUT YOU, but I have grown weary of the self-improvement project. The endless quest to uncover and slay the host of inner demons who have been messing up my plans for enlightenment, which I have imagined as some pure land of perfect equanimity in which I hover over my worldly concerns like a cartoon yogi, forever free from narcissism and other embarrassing inclinations, reliably dispensing compassion to the vulnerable, wisdom to the ignorant, and a kind of sexy psychic luminescence to anyone who comes into proximity with my purified and perfected (no)self.

It hasn't been fruitful, anyway. The same rage arises when I'm bombarded with three competing demands at once, for example, attempting to compose a politically delicate email whilst my dogs are barking their heads off outside my window and I've just knocked over my cup of tea. I still lose it. I holler and pound my desk, sending my little statues of Saraswati and Our Lady of Guadalupe toppling. It's not pretty.

Not to minimize my neuroses. They get a lot worse than this. A stew of bad behaviors stemming from contradictory thought patterns: I'm too much; I'm not enough; nobody sees me; everyone wants something from me; why does so-and-so get all the spiritual accolades when this is my area of expertise? I indulge myself in mini tantrums or cold shoulders, demands for other people's attention or ghosting those who irk me. I despair of ever rising above this quagmire.

Along comes Matt Licata's compassionate book, *A Healing Space*. In these pages, Matt, with exquisite patience, warmth, and poetry, invites us to enter and inhabit the darkness in our souls as holy ground. He tenderly guides us to show up in our bodies, connected by our breath, and begin to consider the possibility of befriending the parts of ourselves we have abandoned, deemed shameful and unworthy, "unspiritual." He lifts the veil from the face of our suffering to reveal the luminous beauty that abides there. He encourages us to share the truth of our shattering so that we become a kind of alchemical vessel in this world, a "healing space" in which others may experience their own transfiguration. Matt affirms that each of us has access to "the outrageous intelligence and bravery of the broken human heart" and the privilege of modeling the heart's ability to return home.

This homecoming, Matt shows us, is probably not what we thought it would be when we signed up for the enlightenment track. We have been conditioned by our spiritual communities—whether traditional religious institutions or alternative practice spaces—to conquer certain feeling states in favor of some idealized realm where we are unmoved by these "lower vibrations," free to claim to our birthright of peace, love, and bliss. Matt points out that this "aggressive campaign against various unwanted bands of the emotional spectrum" pushes a vast array of meaningful, intelligent, and valid energies into the shadows where they will spill from the seams of our strained psyches and cause even more suffering, to ourselves and to others.

What if, instead of rushing to our meditation cushion or asana practice like a grim soldier stepping onto the battlefield, ready to vanquish the ego once and for all, we take our ego into our arms and lean close and hear the wisdom at the core of its insistent lament? How about we enter into psychotherapy like a mother putting aside her endless to-do list and settling down to play with her toddler, driven by no other agenda than loving curiosity? Could we pray the prayers and serve the marginalized and work for peace and justice not to clean up our karma or grease the gates of heaven but rather as a lived recognition of our participation in the web of interbeing that connects us all?

One of my favorite parts of *A Healing Space* is in the teachings of alchemy. I have always been fascinated by the metaphor of transmuting the lead of our difficult experiences into something golden, whether a work of art or a life of service. But in this book, Matt offers a much deeper and more revolutionary aspect of the alchemical process that I ever imagined: the ancient alchemists did not view the base material as merely something to be transcended or gotten rid of, but as "the substance of the gods." Sacred. Beautiful. *Loveable.* In fact, upon committing themselves to the vessel of transmutation, they entered into what Matt calls "a love affair with reality." What would it look like, Matt asks us, if we were to love our heartbreak, our sadness, our confusion? Let's add to that list: our depression, our envy, our shame? If we were to love reality however it is appearing in this moment. Alchemical transmutation! Warmed by the fire of our own tenderness, held safely in the vessel of loving inquiry.

What a revolutionary take on healing! Rather than muscle our way through spiritual disciplines and therapeutic interventions, we fall in love with our brokenness at last and welcome all the orphaned parts of ourselves home.

It takes a combination of courage, hard work, patience, and trust to meet our shadow, lift it to the light, and allow it to integrate with the rest of our being as we rewire our brains and recalibrate our lives. The parts of ourselves we've so desperately tried to banish, which keep dragging their asses back at most unwelcome hours, once served a useful purpose and deserve to be met with a degree of kindness and appreciation.

But it's difficult to do shadow work alone. A few years ago, when I was first being called to step up as a public figure on the spiritual circuit, I was in turmoil. I was moody and ungrounded and felt like a spiritual fraud. Part of me was thrilled that everything I had so passionately cared about all my life finally mattered to the world, and the other part of me wanted to run and hide. I was simultaneously plagued by insecurity and annoyed by what I perceived to be false projections of my ability to save people's souls. Something in me was about to die, I could feel it, and I was both attracted and terrified by the prospect.

Enter Matt Licata. I had the good fortune of being introduced to this gentle master of the human heart at a time when he was still offering one-on-one counseling. Matt created a safe container for me to enter the hot heart of my seemingly most intractable fears and sorrows. This was not some kind of spiritual boot camp, but rather an opportunity to lovingly welcome my own death, as the mystics I write about have celebrated in poetry and song, and emerge with the capacity of the heart to offer of myself as a "healing space" for others. Matt didn't underestimate what would be required of me as I navigated the depths of darkness—not only the shadow parts of myself but the vast holy mystery itself—and yet he did not abandon me for a moment. His calm and kindly presence, his respectful holding, emboldened me to take the risk of offering myself to the flames of my own alchemical transmutation. Nor was this a one-time event that ended when our therapeutic relationship came to a close. It is an ongoing process of befriending myself and recognizing the face of the sacred everywhere, not in spite of but as the fruit of suffering, both my own and the pain of the world.

Just as we have always suspected, this soul work is not an individual task, and we are not alone. "Behind the scenes," Matt writes in this magnificent book, "love is at work, the beloved spinning out worlds of experience, longing to know itself through form, finding illumined passage through us as vessels of light and dark." Whenever we show up for each other and bear witness, blessing each unique version of the human predicament, soothing one another's overwrought nervous systems with our loving presence, we provide safe passage, Matt assures us, and "together we break more, burn more, and somehow become more whole."

INTRODUCTION

An Invitation into a Healing Space

AT SOME POINT ALONG THE WAY, each of us will be asked to revision the ideas that have accompanied us to this moment in our lives. Although at times the call arrives quietly and slowly, as a whisper guiding us into new territory, for many it comes as an unexpected visitor, erupting in the night as we find ourselves in transition, confused, angry, heartbroken, uncertain, or depressed. However it arrives, it is a reminder that even our most sacred identities and beliefs tend to become encrusted over time, worn-out symbols of a living reality no longer so alive. Somehow what was clear only days or even moments ago has lost its meaning and is no longer able to accompany us into the next phase.

The recurring theme we will explore in this book is how we can meet the challenges of life in a new way imbued with curiosity, wisdom, and compassion. In replacing the old circuitry of shame, self-aggression, and self-abandonment with holding, kindness, and attunement, we discover the sacredness of "ordinary" life, which turns out not to be so ordinary after all. In this unearthing, even our most difficult, confusing, and painful experiences are filled with intelligence and in some unexpected way turn out to be guardians on the path. As we make the journey together, we will uncover and experiment with new perspectives, tend mindfully and with tenderness to our immediate experience, and discover fresh layers of purpose and meaning.

A *Healing Space* is not a book to read cover to cover in one sitting or to struggle to understand conceptually but to pick up from time to

1

time in response to an inner call. I hope that it inspires you to slow down and listen to the unique invitation being presented to you at this precise moment in your life. Trust your intuition and internal guidance system as you decide which chapters to focus on, read a few paragraphs, put the book down often, and allow yourself to be moved from within as you meet with new images, feelings, and discoveries. I love the idea of you taking the book out into nature, to sit on the earth and ask her to choose the page, the paragraph, and the guidance for which your soul is thirsty. Read the book not only with an open, critical mind but with your entire body, the softness of your heart, and the creativity of your imagination. Let it penetrate you, cell by cell. There is no need to struggle to "understand" every word in some linear, rational way, but I invite you to enter a visionary world with the ideas, emotions, and images evoked, making a journey with them as kindred travelers of the mystery.

My words are more *poetic* than *prescriptive*, meaning I will not lead you step-by-step through too many exercises or provide detailed instructions. There are many gifted teachers and guides of meditation, prayer, visualization, and deep inner work from whom you might benefit along the way. Rather, my intention is that the book be a companion during times of darkness, confusion, and uncertainty, or in *any* moment when you find yourself longing for inspiration, depth, and perspective. It's not intended to be a substitute for your direct experience, but a caring friend, a whisper inviting you back home, which in some paradoxical way you have never truly left.

Although I hope to invite you into deeper participation in the mystery as it appears in and as your life, I do not have any answers for you. Rather, I see my role as helping to illuminate the immensity and even magic of the questions themselves. The nature of these questions is unique and communicated in a language and in images created specifically for you. My words are only fingers pointing to a moon already rising within you, and my sole intention is to guide you back into the creativity and intelligence saturating your cells at this very moment, whether you feel worthy of it or believe you are a mess or have totally fallen apart. Even in these moments, you are being held by something vast. Let us provide a temple or sanctuary for your own wisdom-essence to emerge as we go through the book together.

Your journey is unprecedented, and you will likely never be ultimately satisfied by a partial or secondhand path. My aim in this book is to invite you into a radical new level of trust in your own experience and into the courageous hero's or heroine's journey, always shimmering with life as it arises freshly in the here and now.

Throughout A *Healing Space*, I will make use of the language, metaphors, and images of diverse traditions such as alchemy, neuroscience, contemplative spirituality, and the poetic imagination to support our journey into the unknown together. I apologize ahead of time to any actual alchemists, neuroscientists, or scholars of religion (I am none of these) because my engagement with these traditions is often outside convention. I am not asking you to take these images *literally*—I do not myself—but as metaphors pointing to a living reality deep within you. There is no need to adopt any new belief system but only to be curious, to open and play with the language along with me as we dream and imagine together, becoming poets and alchemists of a new world.

By integrating a variety of perspectives into our inquiry, we honor the integrity, complexity, and majesty of the psyche, the infinite nature of the heart, and the vast depths of the soul. Each mode of investigation provides a distinctive lens through which to view and approach the magnificence of life and the vastness that holds us all. Although these various ways of exploring experience are at times contradictory, we can make use of the contradictions to enrich our discoveries and more deeply appreciate how miraculous the human person truly is. In one moment, scientific language might seem the most provocative and attuned, and in the next, meditative, alchemical, or poetic expression will be the doorway we step through together into new perception, openheartedness, and self-discovery.

ALCHEMY AND UNEARTHING LIGHT IN THE DARKNESS

Although you might have some experience with psychological work, mindfulness, and meditation as viable pathways of healing and spiritual development, alchemy and its potential application to our lives in the modern world could be new to you. It is beyond the scope of this book to provide a historical survey of the tradition of alchemy, or any sort of comprehensive investigation of its processes and goals. For our purposes, we will explore alchemy's practical relevance to our primary theme of discovering the sacred within the ordinary and mining the intelligence buried within our symptoms, emotions, and most challenging experience. This is something alchemy is uniquely able to help us with, in ways that might not be immediately apparent. In this way, the entire alchemical "opus" (the word the alchemists used to refer to their work) is an invitation into "a healing space" where each of us is the alchemist of our own lives, conducting and artfully tending to an experiment of creative discovery and the unfolding of soul.

Although at the external level, alchemists were involved with the conversion of base metals into silver or gold, we will focus on relating to our inner experience with an alchemical sensibility, making use of alchemical images, metaphors, language, and processes as rich, evocative lenses through which to approach our lives. In this way, our work will be to convert experience we have deemed painful, problematic, and confusing into wisdom-filled, sacred expressions of our human souls, providing critical guidance and meaning along the way. By doing so, we unearth the *aurum philosophicum* (philosophical gold), or the inner jewels that are buried deep within us. The true alchemist was not interested in converting lead to gold to increase his or her external

4

wealth but to "redeem" the lead to its majestic state, that of spirit. This notion of "redemption" is an important one in alchemy and has parallels in our own lives, where we're invited to "redeem" difficult and challenging experiences in such a way that their wisdom may be revealed—their purpose, meaning, and roles in our own healing.

Although there are many ancient alchemical texts, dating back to early Greek, Egyptian, and Arabic sources, my engagement with alchemy has arisen primarily out of the work of two great contemporary alchemical psychologists, C. G. Jung and James Hillman (see the bibliography for a list of their works cited). I owe a great debt to these two pioneers and explorers, without whom our modern psychological understanding of alchemy would likely not have been possible. Because alchemy is much less familiar than the other streams of inquiry discussed, here I would like to plant a seed for our future explorations together.

THE CREATIVE ROLE OF DISSOLUTION

One of the common ways alchemical work begins is through the operation of *solutio* (solution), where the "stuff," or material, of our lives (i.e., our various life circumstances, relationships, emotional vulnerabilities, health issues, family dynamics, experiences with work and career) dissolves and returns to its "original state."[1] Through this process, it becomes a "solution" in both senses of the word: a liquid that remains after a breakdown of essential elements *and* a response to a challenge. Isolating and working with this "original state" is essential on the journey of transformation, said to take form as a substance the alchemists referred to as the *prima materia*, the most basic "material" we have to work with as archaeologists of the inner world.[2]

This dissolution can express itself through the ending of a relationship or job, for example, or through a depression or dark night, anxiety or other psychological symptoms, vivid fantasies and dreams, difficult emotions or sensations in the body, or existentially through the loss of meaning and purpose. Although we might romanticize this activity as evidence of spiritual opportunity or even as the appearance of grace, it comes with a certain devastation and is not something we are likely to enjoy or call forth voluntarily. This movement in psyche is not oriented in "improving" our lives, helping us adapt or fit in, or in what we would ordinarily think of as "self-development" but as a required darkening we must go through to begin our work anew, with fresh vision.

In contemplating the various *solutio* moments of my own life—the losses and reorganizations I have gone through in my work, family, intimate relationships, and physical health—they were not times of contentment and flow but of revolution, in which I wasn't sure if I would make it through to the other side. In many ways, I did not, at least the "me" who was there at the start of the process. In the same way, as the material in the vessel was worked on by the alchemist—by way of the various processes and operations—it would inevitably change into something else; what the alchemist started with never remained the same and was often rendered completely unrecognizable as it underwent the journey of transmutation. Likewise with our own inner process; there are times when what we have counted on to provide value, certainty, and meaning falls apart and is no longer able to support our deepest attitudes and convictions about ourselves and the world. The reality is that the material of our lives is always in flux. Although it is tempting to view this natural reorganization as an error or mistake, a sign that something has gone "wrong" or that we have failed, this discovery is, paradoxically, the basis for renewal and transformation.

A certain kind of death occurs by way of dissolution, revealing that the process of healing is not *only* a movement of creativity and light but also of destruction and the dark. Part and parcel of this disbanding is the discovery that life is no longer envisioned as something for us to "master" or to "perfect" but to enter afresh in each moment, willing

6

to be awed and surprised at what we discover. There is no final landing place where we can rest free from the possibility that the rug can (and will) be removed from underneath us at any time, exposing dimensions of the soul hidden until now.

It is a humbling path, devastating and illuminating simultaneously. Enlivening and at times disorienting. To paraphrase Jung, making the darkness conscious is not what most of us had in mind when we started the journey.[3] We might wonder from time to time whether this is the path for us, only to remember that we are unwilling to settle for a half-life any longer; only the full spectrum is going to meet the longing placed within us. The call is to a greater light found only in embodied, compassionate tending to the dark in all its forms.

If we do not engage consciously in the process of dissolution (and even if we do), life will bring dissolution *to* us, by way of transition, change, and psychic upheaval of all kinds: the ending of a relationship we thought would last forever, a concerning health diagnosis, the loss of a job, an unexpected depression, or the inability to find meaning in our experience. Without the healing waters of dissolution, we remain stuck in habitual consciousness, subject to the narrow band of the historical lenses through which we have come to perceive self, others, and world. Through the illumination of these lenses we can harness the creative power of the imagination, the wildness of the heart, and the courage and vision to dream a new dream.

INTO UNCHARTED TERRITORY

The purpose of *A Healing Space* is to inspire you to open to the unexpected wisdom, creativity, and beauty in your immediate experience, through the eyes and the heart of the alchemist you are. I hope that it serves as a supportive, attuned guide and friend, inviting you into the experiential realization that you are *not* a project to be solved but a mystery coming into form. How we can best honor that mystery and allow its qualities to inform and illuminate our lives is something we'll be exploring as we make this journey together into uncharted territory. The love of the truth makes the work of the alchemist possible, and it is my intention that through our time together this love will come alive in ways that might surprise you.

It is essential that you have an honest dialogue with yourself about what healing means *specifically* for you; this is where secondhand knowledge and any sort of prefabricated description of the path must be replaced by the fire of direct experience, even when that experience is one of uncertainty, disappointment, hopelessness, and doubt. A recurring theme in A *Healing Space* is that these unwanted visitors are allies in disguise, emissaries of wisdom and creativity sent by psyche to further introduce us to the majesty of what we are. Although we are conditioned to believe that transformation and healing are products of finding the right "answer," the invitation here is to break open to the vastness of the question itself. For here, in this illuminated brokenness, the water of life will be found.

True healing is not a state in which we become liberated from feeling but freer and flexible to experience it more fully. It is the willingness to make a journey into the darker, deeper, more complex, and more nuanced dimensions of the psychic spectrum, to touch the fullness of what it means to have taken birth here, to allow in the implications of this and to use these discoveries to connect with others. Through this exploration, we come to discover that although suffering feels and *is* personal, it is *also* archetypal and, as the Buddha noted, universal in human experience. The invitation is to allow our broken hearts, confused minds, and vulnerable emotional bodies to serve as a bridge to a place where we can make embodied, loving contact with the "others" in our lives—not only the external others but the inner others who have become lost along the way.

Throughout A *Healing Space*, we'll travel together inside our moods, thoughts, fantasies, dreams, memories, imagination, bodies, impulses, and feelings and allow ourselves to be touched by their colors, fragrances, and essences. To do this will require patience and courage, but more than anything a new kind of curiosity and the willingness to take a risk: to dare to see that there is intelligence in our neurosis, wisdom in our symptoms, and sacred data in our emotions. It doesn't mean that we will "like" what we find or that we can or even want to "accept" it, not to mention "love" it. The commitment is to envision our lives in a new way, befriend ourselves and our experience, and no longer abandon ourselves in times of intensity, confusion, and challenge. To discover firsthand the rarity of having a human body, a sometimes-broken heart, and a miraculous, sensitive nervous system. To apprehend the breathtaking reality of a sunset fully experienced, just how astounding it is to have the capacity to listen, feel, sense, weep, fail, and succeed. To fall to the ground and get back up, only to fall again and behold the mercy of that cycle once again.

This exploration is not oriented in transcending our vulnerability—fleeing into a state of power, untouchability, and control—or safely hiding in some protected spiritual cocoon where we've risen above it all. There's no "mastering" here. Life is not something to master but to stand in awe of and participate in. We do this by way of the mind and heart of the beginner, the one who knows it is possible (likely) in any moment for life to reorganize and rearrange all our constructed spiritual identities and fantasies. Life can and will do this, if we're lucky, throughout our entire lives, as it excavates deeper territories of the heart.

It is not about taking refuge in spiritual concepts, even noble ones such as "the present moment" because as we all know we can hide out anywhere, and "the present moment" is no exception. It is a particularly rich and subtle place to hide. But it is pointing to something wilder than that. Something more magical. More raw. *At times, even more painful.* In this revisioning, pain is something we enter consciously, as a curious traveler of the unknown, committed to participate and behold in more and more subtlety and depth the entire range of human experience as it unfolds here.

It's not a life that always feels safe, peaceful, and confirms to our most deeply conditioned hopes, ideas, and dreams. But it is one rooted in creation *and* destruction, dark *and* light, vast enough to hold it all, in which we are able to make use of everything here as a way to penetrate the miracle, to see beyond the veil, and connect more deeply with others, helping them (and ourselves) in ever more creative ways. We enter into the miracle by fully *participating* in life, not only in those known, safe, and secure feelings and experiences but in the entire spectrum, where we might discover an unknown bounty that awaits us. From this perspective, our "life's purpose" is to *live*, fully, and honor the rare opportunity we have been given to have a heart that is sometimes broken and sometimes whole.

A RADICAL APPROACH TO SUFFERING

To see our pain, confusion, and struggle as an intelligent communication from the deepest parts of ourselves is a radical approach, to be sure. To suffer *consciously* is an ancient, sacred art lost in our time, replaced by a well-intentioned, solar self-help industry designed to take us out of the darkness and complexity and into consistent joy, flow, happiness, and bliss. There is nothing wrong, of course, with any of these positive states! Let us rejoice and give thanks when they arrive, but not at the expense of fragmentation, self-abandonment, and the psychic exhaustion of an unending search for improvement. Before we deem other, darker experiences invalid or see them as obstacles to a purposeful and fulfilling life, let us slow down, open, and see. When we experience suffering consciously, it reveals something we might not have expected. The meaning found within conscious suffering continues to be whispered to us by hidden alchemists, yogis, poets, artists, parents, and ordinary women and men if we will but listen to the thundering silence. For in abandonment of the silvery, moon-like essence of the darker shades of the spectrum, we lose touch with vitality, wisdom, and soul.

For some reason, we were given a heart that is whole, and no matter how seductive it can be at times, we will never be satisfied resigning ourselves to that which is partial, even if it does feel a bit more safe and secure. Perhaps this wired-in longing for the full spectrum is a blessing *and* a curse, for at times it can feel overwhelming because the burning can and will incinerate everything that is less than illuminated within us. This incineration is another vital process we can learn about from the alchemists, for like the *solutio*, the *calcinatio* burns and transmutes the raw material into a fine, white powder, into the ashes of new life.[4] We will never feel fully alive through embracing only those feelings, images, dreams, and parts of ourselves that our families, societies, and authorities claim are worthy and valid, but only through the courage required to embrace the entire display, to befriend it all, and to transform the raw material of our lives into the luminous expression of wisdom and love in all its forms.

Together, may we partake of the entirety of the range of this human experience, with as much curiosity, soul, and kindness as we can discover. And may we give ourselves permission to care, to take a risk in allowing one another to matter, and to tend to the heart as it inevitably breaks in response to a bittersweet world—not to *mend* the heart, necessarily, for we are not sure if this is what it truly wants. We must discover the heart's deepest longing and whether it needs repair, even during times when it has been shattered. Or maybe it is crying out for something a bit more magical, more creative, more alive. Maybe at times we need to crumble to the ground at the magnificence of it all, awestruck at the bounty laid out before us. To fall apart. To fail. To get back up. To be humbled again. To start over. To be a beginner. An amateur at the ways of love. To make this journey with our kindred travelers and the sun, moon, and stars. And to realize together how little we know in the face of it all.

Thank you for sharing some of your heart and life with me as we turn toward the mystery together.

MATT LICATA
Autumn 2020
Boulder, Colorado

REIMAGINING WHAT
IT MEANS TO HEAL

IT IS IMPORTANT TO SLOW DOWN and bring new life to the ideas, language, and lenses through which we engage our psychological and spiritual lives. To at times start over, begin anew, and not assume we know too much about the heart and its mysteries. Otherwise, we can find ourselves in an overly abstract relationship with soul and spirit, flattened and uninspired, and out of contact with something dynamic and alive. One concept in deep need of reimagining is that of "healing" itself. In my work as a psychotherapist and with those on longer retreats, underneath the varied experiences and unique life circumstances, nearly everyone I speak with reports a longing to experience *true* healing, whatever that might mean for them, a healing that goes beyond the surface and into the depths—not a temporary fix but a transformation that penetrates to the core.

Many are exhausted by old ways of being and worn-out approaches to enlightenment and improvement, frustrated with not being able to bring forth a life they know is possible, based on the deepest truths they have discovered. But all too frequently, the concept of healing becomes generalized and theoretical and loses its vitality. Perhaps it was once associated with a creative, transcendent vision of life but over time has become just another word among many, a distant goal and faraway dream, devoid of the meaning and possibility it once had. It has become experience-distant, pointing to some vague sense of a life without disturbance, free from emotional intensity, reliably certain and safe, in which we dwell outside history and time in a realm filled with consistent feelings of peace, bliss, and spiritual insight. Although this all sounds good on the outside, somehow the lived reality of "healing" has lost its potency and promise.

What people often mean by "healing" is a permanent condition in which we will no longer have to be in direct contact with certain experiences we do not like, ones that we are unable to manage and control or that in some way represent a sense of failure to us. Healing then becomes a way of protecting ourselves from the ever-alive reality of our own vulnerability, not knowing, and the mysteries of life. The underlying belief is that if we can "heal," then we will be able to avoid the uncertainty. Even if we might not be consciously aware of these ideas about healing, for many of us they color our perception under the surface.

As we penetrate the deeper layers of our experience, which we'll do as we make our way through this book together, we might discover ways we've come to imagine "healing" as a condition in which we'll never again be asked to confront disappointment, confusion, depression, shame, fear, or the reality of a vulnerable, shattered heart. The absence of certain feeling states would be clear evidence that we have "healed" and can now get on with our lives. *But is this healing or is it fear?* This largely unexamined view of healing, which tends to operate subtly and for the most part outside conscious awareness, sets up a situation in which we are subtly in resistance to life. It can be revealing to discover how our ideas about healing are tangled up in the fear and avoidance of certain experiences, in staying out of those human states of disappointment, uncertainty, and not knowing. If fear is the guiding energy behind the activity to replace one experience with another, are we actually healing or just furthering our own entrenchment in the energy of fear itself?

If, for example, each time anger—or jealousy, grief, sadness, or confusion—arises in our experience, we make a move to replace it with happiness, gratitude, or joy, and the anger temporarily "goes away," is this healing? Or is it something else? I am suggesting that any activity of self-abandonment takes us away from true healing, fueled by fear and the deeply wired-in belief that we cannot stay close and befriend ourselves in the face of certain challenging emotional experience. We've fallen out of touch with the wisdom inherent in the difficulties of life, which is understandable. But we're going to reexamine this together, slowly and provocatively, and step back into the unknown, where the mystery awaits us.

Throughout *A Healing Space*, I'll refer often to the idea of "self-abandonment," which points to a whole family of ideas, strategies, and behaviors designed to take us out of the immediacy of our experience, especially difficult *feeling* experience, and describes how we turn from ourselves in difficult times. When we abandon ourselves, we often fall down a rabbit hole of dissociation, denial, shame, judgment, and blame and lose touch with the valid, human, and honorable inner experience that longs for our attention, curiosity, and care. I'll be saying a lot more about self-abandonment in future chapters because untangling it is one of the core foundations of a profound transformation and healing and the encoding of new circuitry woven of the substances of curiosity, empathy, and self-realization.

The challenge with our conditioned strategies of self-abandonment is that they *are* effective, in a way. They do seem to work . . . well, sort of. At least they *appear* effective in the moment because they can help remove us temporarily from some shaky territory. We can see our various forms of addiction, for instance, as expressions of self-abandonment, as ways to avoid feeling states we have come to associate with something incredibly unsafe, unworkable, embarrassing, or seen as evidence that there is something wrong with us. For example, eating when we're not hungry; unconscious use of television or the internet; unhealthy sexual expression; or harmful dependency on drugs, alcohol, or even another person, especially when that person is unkind to us. Perhaps we've trained ourselves to control and manage our lives so that they're okay; things might be relatively certain and safe. But we might also feel dead, flat, and frozen, with a vague sense that something is missing. Even if we can't put our finger on it, it haunts us as a ghost of our unlived lives. What is it?

When all is said and done, we must set aside *all* outside definitions of healing (including the ones in this book!) and turn home, back into the fire of our own direct experience. For only there can we discover for ourselves what healing is, its unique meaning and expression in our lives, our motivations for wanting to heal, and the ways we might unconsciously be resisting the changes we know will be required. This inquiry around the nature of what true healing means specifically *for us* is one we are each invited to engage slowly, with curiosity, to sit with patiently, yielding as it penetrates us cell by cell. We have to allow ourselves to return to the openness of the amateur, take the risk of stepping into the unknown, and start afresh. We can burn in the sacredness and purity of the questions and resist the temptation to scramble into answers for which we might not be prepared or that belong to another. One of the core aspirations of this book is to hand this holy task back to you, the reader, to support and empower you to make the journey for yourself and to discover your own subtleties and truths about these matters, so sacred, personal, and poetic that only you can decipher them.

THE CONTRADICTORY NATURE OF HEALING

To discover the nature of healing for ourselves, we must open and listen to previously unacknowledged parts of the psyche; otherwise we will be in touch only with what we *already know*. One of the core premises of this book is that true healing and transformation are in large part discovered in the unknown—in those unfamiliar voices, thoughts, feelings, and images that dwell deeper in the soul, in those realms of experience not always lit by conscious awareness. Although a part of us genuinely wishes to heal, awaken, and transform, there are lesser known, hidden parts that have an unconscious investment in maintaining things the way they are.[1] The momentum to preserve the status quo, emotionally and otherwise, is deeply embedded, and we must never take for granted the power of the pull back into the way things have always been. Throughout the book, we will illuminate and provide sanctuary for these concealed parts, explore how and why they have become so established in our experience, and how we can befriend and illuminate them, ultimately recognizing their true nature as allies and helpers. These shadowy figures and energies speak throughout the day and night, not to harm us or provide unnecessary obstacles to overcome but as invitations into depth, as guides, messengers, and emissaries of the vastness of what we are. But in order to discover this for ourselves, we must cleanse our perception, untangle the pathways, and begin to imagine ourselves and the world in a radically new way.

We can hear these voices, for example, as they make themselves known through questions such as: Why, after years or even decades of working on myself, meditating, praying, surrendering, and going to therapy can it seem like nothing is changing? Why do I keep choosing an unavailable partner? How can this grief still be here? Why am I depressed? When will I ever find meaningful work? Why I am always feeling disappointed or disappointing others? When will the feelings of shame, unworthiness, and rage go away? When do I reach the end, become fully awakened, enlightened, totally healed? When will it change? Will this burning ever be resolved; will the longing ever be fulfilled? As these and similar questions come into our conscious awareness throughout the day and night, the veiled parts of ourselves make their way into the light, the lost and orphaned ones of the soul reach out to us in the hope of reunion, where we can finally tend to them with curiosity, awareness, and compassion. Through our willingness to touch and be touched by them, they are able to find their rightful place in the greater ecology of what we are.

Learning to contact and bring illumination to those parts terrified of and resistant to healing and change is an act of profound kindness, though this task is often overlooked as part of our inner work. It is natural to provide a home for ideas and aspects of ourselves that align with the ways we want to be seen, that support our fantasy that we're consistently in control of all aspects of our lives. But when it comes to other voices that do not line up with who we think we are, who we want to be, or how we want to be seen by others, we understandably run into resistance. We defend against these figures and energies, abandon them when they appear, and send them into the shadow, where they will continue to try to reach us in ever creative (and often disturbing) ways. I'll have a lot more to say about the shadow and unacknowledged soul parts in chapter 8.

As we begin to listen carefully to the differentiated voices and parts of ourselves that have something to say about the process of transformation, we encounter one of the most subtle and powerful discoveries of this work: the foundation of reorganizing our experience and manifesting true healing is in a radical new revisioning of friendship with ourselves. Sufi tradition speaks eloquently and poetically about the nature of this "Friend," the mysterious "other" who longs for relationship with us at all times, pointing to the mystery of friendship and its role on the path of awakening. This Friend can appear as an internal or external other and draws us into itself—into union, discovery, meaning, and light. True friendship must not only involve those parts that are positive, flowy, and confirming of who we think we are but perhaps even more importantly those with which we are not so familiar or repelled by, those that run counter to the image we have of ourselves. In ways often contradictory to the one seeking control and maintenance of the status quo, the radical act of befriending *all* parts of ourselves is what makes true healing possible. It is important to realize and respect how revolutionary this is—the journey to reverse years, decades, and perhaps even lifetimes of habitual, conditioned patterning of repressing parts of ourselves and placing them into the darkness, where they have no choice but to reach out from the shadows to find us once again. More poetically, the Friend misses us, and we miss him or her; we long to be together again, dancing and playing in unstructured states of being, awareness, and love.

HEALING WILL ALWAYS SURPRISE US

Although we can honor the authentic call to transformation—those voices, images, and parts of ourselves that genuinely want to heal—we must also be prepared to confront the real-world implications of what all this will inevitably require, which can be life-shattering. For when we heal, the way we have come to organize our experience—the things we like to do, the people we find ourselves drawn to, the familiar reference points that provide our identity—tend to fall apart. But this "falling apart" is a sacred process, evidence of the critical alchemical operation of *putrefactio*, or putrefaction, in which the known crumbles and disintegrates, revealing important and lesser-known dimensions of our experience not available during times of clear reflection and "holding it all together." These old, inner soul companions can no longer be accessed and used in the same way, to locate ourselves and confirm who we think we are and what will fulfill our deepest longing. They just can't contain us any longer; they're not subtle, nuanced, or magnificent enough. To transmute our lives in this way might sound inspiring on the surface, even thrilling (sign me up!), but remember, *true transformation is destructive as well as creative* and does not always conform to the ways we thought it would all turn out. In other words, healing *will* surprise us.

For example, if we fully transform our shame and unworthiness and heal from that deeply rooted sense that something is wrong with us at the most basic level, what will our lives be like? What will our relationships be like? How will we interact with others if not through these painful wounds of a lifetime? Who will we be; how will we live, move, and have our being? If those familiar lenses are no longer available, how will we see and navigate? What will we organize around? What is the axis around which we will orient? What will be the new image, metaphor, or lens through which we engage?

Many I have worked with over the years have come to discover the great liberation in the realization that they are not who they thought they were, as well as the profound disorientation of losing their familiar reference points in the aftermath of a profound healing or awakening experience. It's important that we honor both of these events, the freeing and liberating nature as well as the existential and primordial confusion that can arise in the wake of healing. One of the mysteries of this work is that we cannot know in advance what it will be like to live our lives without our conditioned ways of seeing the world. If we set our glasses down (or if they are removed by life or God or spirit or soul), we will be required to see with new vision, unable to depend on the known to guide us in the way it used to. This can be a profoundly contradictory place to find ourselves. Yes, there is a certain excitement in stepping into new territory, but it can also generate bewilderment or even panic because we sense a pending confrontation with the unknown. We must be kind to ourselves during times of transition, honoring the actualities of what it truly means to heal. We must slow down and soften as we are asked to provide sanctuary for the wounds, grief, and unfelt joys of a lifetime and offer a temple of rest where the disowned inner travelers can gather and return.

TURNING THE HEART

As we move into this enlivened new territory, we open the doorways (in some cases floodgates) for reunion with unknown aspects of ourselves, as well as the survival-level anxiety our defensive organization has successfully kept at bay for so long.[2] It's literally impossible to know what this will be like, but we sense the implications, I believe, at a deep level. This core sensing gives rise to the part of us that feels contradictory when it comes to healing, convinced that maintaining things as they are—even if "as they are" is less than ideal, flat, overly protected, and uninspiring—is the safest bet, the surest way to stay out of overwhelming feeling and the exposure of too much vulnerability.

Facilitating a dialogue between these various voices can help us to make sense of this paradoxical territory, where we listen compassionately to both sides and come to deeper understanding of their perspectives and concerns. This way, when either side surges in a here-and-now moment, we are prepared to meet whatever thoughts and feelings come our way and not judge or attack ourselves in the face of the perceived inconsistency. If we do not provide a sanctuary for those voices that genuinely desire healing *as well as remain in resistance to it*, it is likely we will conclude that the conflicting energies are evidence of some problem or that somehow we have failed. We can cut into this habitual conclusion by training ourselves to *expect* to feel this way, not falling into the trap of shame and blame when the contradictions inevitably arise, and staying committed to befriend whatever appears as best we can. Although providing an accepting home for the uncertainty might not be something we ever *want* to do, true healing is not possible without tending to our essential vulnerability and the entirety of unfelt feelings and aspects of ourselves we have kept out of conscious awareness. It is not possible for us to awaken and transform our lives without befriending all parts of ourselves, calling them all back home into the larger field of what we are.

As we allow ourselves to honor these contradictions, to see them as natural and even intelligent and holy, we realize at deeper and deeper levels that healing is not a process of eradicating the unwanted and sending it into the shadow, but it is attunement to the *entirety* of what we are. By deserting that which longs for reunion, we create the conditions for future eruption, which is sure to occur in less-than-conscious ways. The invitation, then, is to cultivate a *conscious* relationship with even our most disturbing and challenging experience, which paradoxically opens us to a larger, more spacious perspective that can make use of whatever arises as "food" or energy for deeper layers of healing. We will never reorganize the patterns of a lifetime by means of self-aggression, which only reinforces the realities of early empathic failure and the shame that arose from the deep sense there is something fundamentally wrong with us.

Increased awareness is critical and necessary, but for most it is not enough to shift the intergenerational trances of habitual consciousness. Many of us have quite a lot of insight into our embedded patterns and "know" what we need to do to heal, to awaken, to transform. But despite all this "knowing," fundamental change can remain elusive. At some point it might only be a turning of the heart that has the power and beauty and poetic impact to soothe the cosmic exhaustion, wounds, and pain of an unlived life, where love is revealed to be the ultimate medicine, which can penetrate the deepest layers of our conditioning and felt sense of separation.

What this "turning of the heart" looks and feels like for each of us must be discovered in the fire of our own direct experience. To open to our pain, our grief, and our longing and allow the allies to reveal themselves requires that we work not only at the level of clear seeing but also at that of deep feeling and honoring of the psyche and soul, including a new valuing of our sensitivities, eccentricities, and unique symptoms. It's important to remember that for most of us, mere insight alone will not reveal the deepest layers of transformation and healing we long for but instead the awareness illumined from within by the heart, by warmth, and by love.

The ancient alchemists were great models of this because the relationship they had with their materials was akin to a love affair. It was hot and intimate and alive. It was painful, heartbreaking, chaotic, and glorious. They allowed the material to matter to them. They loved the minerals and vessels and fires—and related to them as living beings they cherished. For them there was no solid dividing line between matter and spirit.

These are all metaphors for how we might tend to our own inner experience—the "matter" of our thoughts, feelings, and sensations—practicing intimacy with the emotional world and the varied experiences that come to us as we commit to the alchemical opus of our own lives.

METABOLIZING EXPERIENCE

In order to know and befriend ourselves at the deepest levels, one of the core foundations for true healing, we must cultivate a new way of relating with ourselves that allows even our most difficult and challenging experience to disclose its meaning, intelligence, and purpose in our lives. To do this, we have to slow down and shift our relationship from one of thinking *about* our experience to *fully embodying it.* We have to allow ourselves to truly touch it and be touched by it rather than merely orbiting around it, where we are sure to continue to feel some degree of disconnection. Just as we must properly digest the food we eat to absorb its nutrients, we must also assimilate our experience to receive the wisdom and sacred data within it. All through the day and night, we are receiving impressions—through our mental, emotional, somatic (i.e., body-based), imaginal, and spiritual bodies. Life is a constant stream of experience—conversations with friends, caring for our kids, cooking a meal, wandering in nature, practicing yoga or meditation, engaging our work and creative projects, reading a book, shopping for groceries, running errands. But to what degree are we *experiencing* all of this? How present are we to our moment-to-moment experience, embodied and engaged, allowing it to penetrate us, where it can become true *experience* and not just some passing event? To what degree are we on autopilot as we make our way through the day, only partially connecting with our friends and family and engaging the sensory reality of what we see, hear, smell, taste, and touch?

I'm pointing toward a way of "metabolizing" our experience that allows us to touch and engage it at the most subtle levels, where it is able to disclose its qualities, intelligence, and purpose. By evoking "metabolization," I am making use of a biological process in a metaphorical way to refer to working through and integrating our experience, especially those thoughts, feelings, sensations, and parts of ourselves that historically we have pushed away. Other words from the biological sciences, for example "digestion," "absorption," or "assimilation" can be used to point to the same idea, indicating that it requires concentration, attention, and a certain fire or warmth to "make use" of our experience and mine the "nutrients" contained within it.

Just because we "have" an experience does not mean we properly digest and absorb it. If our emotional and sensory experience remain partly processed, they become leaky (a psychic version, if you will, of "leaky gut syndrome") and unable to provide the fuel required to live a life of intimacy, connection, and spontaneity. This inner psychic situation is analogous to not properly chewing and breaking down the food we eat and thus not being able to mine the energy and nutrients our bodies need to function optimally.

Although the desire for change and transformation is natural, noble, and worthy of our honor and attention, if we are not careful, it can serve as a powerful reminder and expression of the painful realities of materialism and self-abandonment. One of the shadow sides of spiritual seeking and the (seemingly) endless project of self-improvement is that we never slow down enough to digest what we have *already* been given, often much more than we consciously realize. In some sense, most of us *have* been given everything in terms of the basic alchemical *prima materia* required to live a life of integrity and inner richness, but not the "everything" the mind thinks it needs to be happy and fulfilled, found by way of a journey of internal and external consumerism. And not the "everything" that conforms to our hopes, fears, and dreams of power and control and that keeps us consistently safe and protected from the implications of what it means to have a tender (and breakable) human heart, but the "everything" *already here* as part of our true nature, the raw materials for a life of inner contentment and abundance, revealed by way of slowness and humility, not unconscious acquisition.

It is important to remember that for most of us, healing happens gradually, slowly, over time when we begin to perceive ourselves and our lives in a new way. Each micromoment of new insight, understanding, and perspective must be integrated and digested on its own, honored and tended to with curiosity, care, and attention. Before we "move forward" to the next moment, we must fully apprehend and open our hearts to this one; this slow tending (metabolization) is one of the true essences of a lasting, transformative, and deep healing. If we are not able to metabolize even our most intense and disturbing experience, we will remain in opposition to it, at subtle war with it, and not able to be in relationship with it as a healing ally.

In Tibetan tradition, there is an image of the hungry ghost, a figure of the imaginal realms with a large, distended belly and tiny mouth. No matter how much food (experience) is consumed, there is a deep ache and longing for more. Regardless of how much is taken in, the ghost retains an insatiable hunger. Because this one is not able to digest, make use of, or enjoy what is given, a primordial hole is left behind that can never seem to be filled. One invitation, as this image appears in our own lives, is to slow way down and send awareness and compassion directly *into* the hole, infusing it with presence and warmth, and finally tend to what is *already* here, not what is missing and might come one day in the future by way of further procurement.

Just as with food—choosing wisely, chewing mindfully, allowing ourselves to taste the bounty of what is being offered, and stopping before we are full—we can honor the validity, workability, and intelligence of our inner experience, even if it is difficult or disturbing. The willingness to fully digest our own vulnerability, tenderness, confusion, and suffering is an act of love and fierce, revolutionary kindness. There are soul nutrients buried in the food of our embodied experience that yearn to be integrated, metabolized, and assimilated in the flame of the heart. But this digestion requires the enzymes of presence, embodiment, compassion, and curiosity about what is here now.

Let us slow down and become mindful of the ways we seek to fill the empty hole in the center, whether it be with food when we're not hungry or experience when we are already full. And in this way, we can walk lightly together in this world, on this precious planet, not as hungry ghosts desperate to be fed but as kindred travelers of interior wealth, richness, and meaning.

LAYERS OF METABOLIZATION

In a spiraling and nonlinear way, the process of metabolization seems to loosely unfold in layers and stages we cannot really skip.[3] We can *try* to skip them, which many of us will naturally attempt to do, but this usually results in further suffering and struggle for ourselves and others. I will discuss in detail in chapter 7 "bypassing" certain aspects of our experience to avoid difficult thoughts and feelings. Rather than shaming or attacking ourselves for seeking a shortcut, or faster or safer way, we can use this discovery to go deeper. The alchemists realized, often through perilous trials and tribulations, that they could not move on to the next phase of their work until the first was completed, or at least understood, in great detail. If we skip over the critical stages of dissolution, deflation, and differentiation, we're not going to be able to fully realize and navigate future operations such as coagulation, synthesis, and unity.

Although it is increasingly common in psychological and spiritual teachings to "accept" and even "love" our deepest fears, vulnerabilities, and shortcomings, it might be naive to believe we can do so without first meeting the material as it is, without any further agenda to transform it into something else. There must be some prerequisite tending of the material with warmth, curiosity, and interest, so that we can get to know it and its qualities, before we open our hearts to it. That sort of artful patience and slowness is a great act of kindness that we can bring to the work and not force ourselves to "love," "accept," or "forgive" before it is indicated and before we have fully touched and been touched by the pain, grief, confusion, vulnerability, and sensitivity with us in the vessel. By slowly and carefully relating to the "material" of our emotional experience in this way, we further the process of its digestion and metabolization. When we encounter the material of our lives in an embodied, mindful, and curious way, we can then see the fears, vulnerabilities, and shortcomings for what they are, feel their qualities and textures, explore their subtleties and nuances, and discover that although they might appear as obstacles to what we most deeply long for, they are actually portals and passageways into it, disclosing more nuanced depth and soul.

As the alchemists discovered, we must first *separate* from the content so that we can enter into relationship with it, where we can see it clearly and differentiate its various components, qualities, and essences. We want to get close but not so close that we merge with the material and become fused, thereby losing perspective. We want to feel its textures and how it comes to us in a moment of activation, or being triggered, genuinely interested in knowing it at the deepest possible level, not as an enemy from the outside but as a part of us that longs to return home. The alchemical process of *separatio* is critical in

27

our coming to know the material in this way, practicing intimacy but not becoming flooded or enmeshed. The potential confusion between *me* and the *material* is something both meditative and alchemical traditions have noted, tracked, and attempted to illuminate in their work.

We cannot expect to move directly from a triggered state of overwhelm into acceptance and love, for this would require that we circumvent the critical stages of getting to know the material first, discovering its qualities and fragrances, its validity and the adaptive role it might still play in our lives. It is honorable to aspire to acceptance and love as noble virtues and goals; however, these experiences remain disembodied concepts until they arise organically as the result of tending to the pain, grief, and emotional vulnerability existing just under the surface. As long as there is an unconscious motivation to work with the material *solely* so that it will be purged from our experience, it is unlikely we'll be able to get close enough for it to be thawed out and clarified by the warmth of the heart.

Initially, we must train ourselves to stay with the intensity for short periods of time, checking in for a few moments in provocative but not traumatizing ways, pushing ourselves a little in a way that does not overwhelm us but builds our resourcefulness and resilience, and allowing ourselves to touch those parts of us that have felt unapproachable and unsafe in the past. Here, *slow is good* because it increases our tolerance for emotional and somatic intensity bit by bit over time. There's no rush to the finish line or shaming ourselves because the process is taking "too long" or we're not doing it right. There is no "too long" in the heart, in the soul, and in the nervous system, only just long enough.

COMPASSIONATE RETRAINING

To reacquaint ourselves with the ways of being, feeling, and perceiving we have historically disavowed takes practice and compassionate retraining of our nervous system to tolerate and contain that which at one time was not possible. It is not a project to rush through or attack ourselves for not doing fast enough, some new goal to add to our spiritual to-do lists. The process has its own timeline, which is unique for each of us and must be respected. The urge to "get in there" and heal everything quickly is not usually an expression of true self-compassion but a leftover remnant of the way our families of origin might have reacted to our emotional experience when we were young children; that is, it's wrong, bad, not okay, and inappropriate and must be dealt with (eliminated, repressed) immediately.

Slowly, we might discover that over time we can endure this material and begin to breathe life back into those parts of ourselves where breath was once not available. We can unfreeze the body, the heart, and parts of ourselves we have closed down to keep us safe. Although it might *feel* otherwise in the moment, it is possible to realize in an experiential way (not just by taking another's word for it or through conceptual understanding only) that staying with an intense feeling for a few seconds is *not* an actual threat to our survival. *This alone is a profound realization that should not be taken lightly.* Somehow, in a way that might surprise us, we are able to meet and make room for experience we were convinced would take us down. Although we might attempt to convince ourselves that "a few seconds" is insignificant, that is not accurate. Seconds at a time weave the neural scaffolding that supports lasting transformation.

Before we can begin to move deeper into areas of acceptance, love, and forgiveness, we must first come to know in a personal and embodied way that staying with what was once unbearable is not going to drop us into an unworkable state of anxiety. This requisite sense of safety is an experience that cannot be skipped; otherwise, it is likely we'll end up reinforcing old patterns of self-aggression and even violence. Historically, lacking in certain capacities to keep ourselves regulated, we had to do whatever it took to escape the fire and get back quickly to safe ground, even if doing so required that we abandon ourselves and enter states of dissociation. It was the wisest choice in the moment, and we can be grateful that we had the wherewithal to make such a decision (even if unconscious), which not everyone is able to do. Although the activity of repression generally carries a negative connotation, it is a developmental achievement that occurs early in our lives, and for those unable to employ dissociative strategies, the consequences can be quite grave. If we allowed in every thought, feeling, emotion, and memory that exists in implicit form in any particular moment, we would find ourselves in a threatening and unmanageable place.

COMING CLOSER TO THE MATERIAL

After we have the repeated experience that we can withstand small doses of intensity as it takes form as activated thought and feeling, we can then begin to increase our tolerance and stay for two seconds instead of one, or ten instead of five, and so forth. Please note that I'm referring to *seconds* here, not minutes or hours. In this way, we move from tolerating the material to starting to contain and hold it, slowly discovering capacities that might not have been available even weeks or months ago. Even if only in a small way, this discovery begins to open our hearts. We naturally become more curious, wanting to care for ourselves in a new way, which "heats up" the material in the vessel and allows us to move closer.

After the intensity is a bit more contained and we are further confident we can stay for short periods of time without falling apart, we discover the safety and permission to continue into more open and undefended dimensions of our experience, including starting to *accept* what has come. By "accept" here, it's important to note we are not condoning or settling for something, resigned to it staying forever, or even making some claim that we "like" what is happening—that we are "okay" with it or have forgiven another for causing us pain. But we start to recognize a deep desire (and capacity) to no longer abandon *ourselves* and our immediate experience, even if we deem it less than ideal. We are willing to experience what has come, to go through it and not around it, for we sense that resisting what is—what in psychological literature is referred to as *experiential avoidance*—is the root cause of so much of our emotional suffering.[4] We accept that *this* is the way reality appears in *this* moment, and we do not want to argue with reality any longer, for to do so only increases our struggle.

It is important to note that "accepting" and "not arguing with reality" is primarily an *internal* practice of awareness and compassion, tending with care to the thoughts, feelings, and sensations alive in us in any given moment. It is *not* remaining passive or failing to defend ourselves in the external world. It is not "accepting" neglect, mistreatment, or abuse or "not arguing" with someone hurting us. It is an act of intelligence and integrity to bring forth clear boundaries, say no (at times loudly and forcefully), engage in healthy conflict when necessary, and do what is necessary to protect our own body, psyche, and integrity. In "not arguing" internally, however, we might begin to discover that the act of *self-abandonment* in all its forms *is often more painful than the actual feelings themselves*. This can be quite a realization and can liberate a tremendous amount of energy.

As a way to make this inquiry more personal and alive, you can state (silently or out loud to yourself or another) your own personal aspiration to no longer abandon yourself, to stay close in times of activation, or being triggered, and to befriend yourself and have self-compassion. Please find the words most resonant for you, but as an example you could say, "No, I'm not going to do that any longer. Even though it takes everything in me, and it feels so shaky, uncertain, and potentially unsafe, I am going to embrace my vulnerability and care for it, slowly, and choose a new way. I will be a friend to myself, and I am no longer willing to be an enemy. Even though I will not be perfect at it and will likely fail at times, I will remain steadfast in my commitment to not turn from myself." This is where the work shifts more to that of the heart, where we aren't as focused on clear insight and pure awareness, and we're not walled off and protected as a witness on the sidelines. Rather, we begin to explore what it would mean in real time to open our hearts to our pain, to hold it like a mother or father enveloping their little baby in their arms. Yes, it's risky. Yes, it's hard. Yes, it will ask *everything* of us. But many of us are discovering there is no longer any other choice.

This is a radical revisioning that truly goes against the grain. We start to bring kindness to the feelings, to the parts of ourselves we had to disown at an earlier time, untangling and enlivening them with the warmth of our own presence, which in these moments we need more than ever. From here, we can discover whether there is suffering *inherent* in difficult emotions—whether it's wired into them as an essential part of their nature—or whether *rejection* of them, turning from them, and believing they are evidence there is something wrong with us are the root causes of our struggle. This latter realization is one of the essential discoveries of the meditative traditions: our ultimate freedom is found not in shifting thoughts and feelings, replacing them with more desirable ones but in our relationship to whatever appears. Having the experiential realization that suffering is not inherent in the wave-like appearance of sadness, rage, shame, grief, or confusion can turn our lives upside down as it becomes clear that we do not need to get rid of, change, shift, transform, or even "heal" our emotions to experience freedom and aliveness.

DEEPLY BEFRIENDING THE UNINVITED

Our embodied, experiential journey of befriending just moves on from there, with deeper and more integrated forms of awareness, kindness, and discovery, traveling into the core of whatever arises and touching it with our hearts, warming it with mindful attention, and tending to all parts of ourselves as an organic practice of self-compassion.

Yes, it is a "practice," not some goal we set up that we then shame ourselves for "failing" at—we're ready to end that cycle and replace it with something more creative, more magical, more alive. At the same time, we realize that this alchemical transmutation of the old pathways—replacing the self-abandonment and archaic misperception with the circuitry of empathy, clear seeing, wisdom, and kindness—does seem to take practice, seconds at a time, moment by moment. It rarely just happens on its own.

As we train ourselves in this way, we might notice that it starts to become second nature to stay close in the wake of challenging thoughts and feelings; we just cannot bear to abandon ourselves. Instead we can breathe into what we once deemed invalid, unbearable, and unworkable. We start to discover a certain softness and spaciousness underlying even our most disturbing experience, and we find true refuge not by eradicating the material but by infusing it with deepening levels of loving awareness.

Eventually we might come to appreciate or even *love* our triggers, genuinely wishing to open to them and know their subtleties at deeper and deeper levels, standing in awe of the opportunity to learn more about consciousness as it comes into form. It's as if a child were knocking at the door and just wanting to be let in for a moment, seeking refuge from an exhausting journey, asking for relief from carrying a burden across a lifetime. How would we respond to this little one when he or she appeared—tired, cold, frightened, and lost—just longing for some rest, some affection, and a safe place by the fire? I think many of us have a sense that we would open the door and allow the child inside—feed, clothe, protect, and hold him or her. But it is critical to remember that we cannot "skip" straight to the stages of acceptance and love, although we might have an intention to get there eventually. We must be honest about where we are and our current capacities in the moment. If we move into these areas in a hasty or impulsive way, before we are ready—without first tending to the real hurt, grief, and pain there—we will only entrench ourselves more deeply. To "bypass" the embodied meeting and working through of difficult thoughts, feelings, and sensations—jumping too quickly into acceptance, love, and forgiveness—is one of the more common expressions of *spiritual bypassing*, which I discuss in chapter 7.

As we befriend the uninvited visitors, paying special attention to those parts of ourselves calling out for extra care and attention, it is common to meet with some fear and hesitation. It is natural to want to get rid of this fear because we conclude that its presence is an obstacle in our path. We're not supposed to be scared, are we? Shouldn't we choose love over fear? Isn't fear an expression of a "low vibration"? As always, we must slow down and see through these well-intentioned spiritual aphorisms and get more subtle and nuanced with it all. Perhaps the problem is not fear but again, rejecting it, pathologizing it, and abandoning it as it inevitably comes for a visit. It is understandable to want to "transform" fear, of course, but in my experience, intelligence is embedded within it and a communication is in its core—a wakeup call from a part of us that longs to be known and allowed back home. If we "get rid of" the fear too quickly, without first heating it up in the vessel with curiosity and awareness, we will lose contact with any message or guidance it has for our journey.

To the degree we find ourselves resistant to meeting and befriending our fear, we reinforce our belief in its pathology and unworkability, which only keeps it alive in our psychic organization. Rather than struggle to purge fear (an ordinary human emotion) from our experience, we might experiment, in small doses, with meeting and holding and exploring its contours and textures. We can experiment with calling off the war with fear and providing sanctuary for that fearful little boy or girl within us, where she can be heard, his feelings can be felt, and her underlying core beliefs can be illuminated. We do this so that finally we can know what he or she needs, why the fear has come, and how we can care for this valid part of ourselves in new way. We dare to see what function the fearful one might be playing in our life experience and the guidance and information he or she might have for us. The invitation is to slowly begin to train ourselves to stay with the fear and the inner figures carrying it for so long, to build the resources, scaffolding, and requisite sense of "safe enough" so that we can begin to truly open our hearts to these old companions. We need not be frightened of our fear any longer but enter into relationship with it as a kindred traveler that has taken a challenging or even wrathful form.

In realizing the real-world implications of what it would mean to transform and heal our deepest wounds and misperceptions, we can bring more insight and compassion to our lives through some understanding as to why healing can seem so difficult at times. To honor the inherently contradictory nature of healing, we must slow down, not assume we know what the word "healing" means, and be willing to start anew. As we lay this new foundation, we build the resources required to step into unmapped territory. From this scaffolding we are able to create new pathways of experience that allow for greater flexibility, freedom, and natural joy.

Opening to the possibility that lasting transformation and healing are not as much about *changing* our experience as retraining ourselves to meet it with new levels of curiosity, perspective, and warmth, we start to sense a sacred world that is *always, already here*, not the product of some grand project of self-improvement.

2

ALREADY HELD

*Encoding New Circuitry and
Opening to the Unknown*

IN THIS CHAPTER, WE WILL EXPLORE the image of "holding" in its various dimensions and what it might mean to "hold" our experience, while simultaneously opening to the possibility that no matter what is happening in our lives, we are always "being held" by something greater than ourselves. The image of "holding" is such an evocative one because it calls up not only early personal experience but also archetypal material that expresses this same psychic patterning throughout history and culture, evidence of the ways we human beings have found solace in "being held" by transpersonal figures, energies, and the natural world itself.

In this chapter I speak in a variety of ways about this image of "holding" and why I find it so relevant to transformation and healing. When we are able to "hold" our experience as well as allow ourselves to "be held" by something larger than our personal sense of self, we learn to trust ourselves and the workability of our lives, even in the midst of uncertainty. We become more spontaneous and creative, more flexible, and better able to respond to the challenges life will inevitably provide.

Even if our experience is difficult and confusing, we come to discover it is taking place within a vast context that might be a lot more purposeful and intelligent than it appears. As our trust deepens in the basic wisdom that underlies even our most trying experience, a natural confidence begins to dawn in ourselves and in life.

Over time, as we illuminate and befriend our experience at deeper levels, we invite its meaning and intelligence to disclose itself. We become more familiar with the surrounding field in which our experience appears, a space that is not empty or void but filled with qualities of warmth, integrity, and value. The alchemists referred to this holding vessel as the *vas hermeticum*, a sealed and supportive container in which transformation can occur. We are the material within the *vas*, and we are also the alchemist looking into it. We are the *vas* itself and in the most primordial way the space in which the entire display has appeared, is held, and becomes transmuted from a base, or leaden condition, into something of value such as silver or gold. Again, remember we are relating to these alchemical images *symbolically*, not literally, as metaphors for the transformation of stuck internal experience such as difficult emotions, fixed core beliefs about ourselves and others, frozen sensations in the body, and the density of habitual consciousness more generally.

As a consequence of profound befriending and the corresponding movement in our emotional, mental, physical, and spiritual bodies, our center of gravity can begin to shift into the experiential realization that we are always, already being held. Even during times of intense struggle and suffering, we are contained within something immense and ultimately trustable. In this way, holding is not something we need to create, deserve, or "earn" by way of completing some heroic project of self-improvement or enlightenment. For it is already wired within us.

You might be familiar with the concept of a "holding environment" as elucidated by British psychoanalyst D. W. Winnicott—a warm and poetic description of a relational configuration rooted in empathic attunement and right-brain to right-brain resonance.[1] More simply, a holding environment points to an inner, felt experience in which we are able to be fully ourselves without apology or shame, where our feelings are validated and mirrored back to us, and where we are able to make sense of our lives in a way that promotes an embodied sense of wholeness. In such an environment, we are able to access, articulate, and metabolize inner experience we might previously have had to disown or repress or weren't even aware we were having. It is a vast "field of permission" in which who and what we are is fully welcome to come into being and unfold in a supportive atmosphere of curiosity, warmth, acceptance, and interest. Within such an environment, we do not need to hold back what we are—including our eccentricities, sensitivities, and unique ways of perceiving and making sense of our experience; these are all welcome, contained, and held in the spaciousness of the here and now. We need not exert unnecessary energy to repress parts of ourselves while enacting other, less authentic parts to "fit in"—we're already fully "in," no extra fitting required.

This image of a holding environment is also related to that area of psychology known as attachment theory, which describes the emotional, neurobiological, and even transpersonal bond between two people and how we come to imagine ourselves, others, and the world through our experience *in relationship*. As the foundation of secure attachment, an adequate holding environment provides the rich, creative terrain from which we can explore reality, resting and playing in unstructured states of being. By "secure attachment" I am referring to the capacity to care for ourselves at the deepest levels *and* at times reach out to others when we need help, not falling into an extreme position in which we have to "do it all on our own" or, alternatively, live from a fused place of unhealthy codependence. We are able to assert our needs and make requests of the others in our lives, honoring our interdependency with them while at the same time not placing an undue burden on them to heal and live for us. We can move in either direction, flexibly and in real time, shifting back and forth, depending on our intuitive, felt sense of the situation. From this ground of emotional suppleness, safety, and psychological elasticity, we journey out of the familiar, encounter and experiment with the not yet known, and stay embodied in the full range of human feeling and experience.

For a holding environment to be "good enough," it must consist of qualities of both contact *and* space, woven together in an optimal and artistic way in which we're able to navigate that fertile middle territory where there is intimacy without fusion.[2] Without adequate contact and without the space in which our natural being can unfold, we lose touch with the mystery—with the vastness of life beyond what we *already* know—with the quantum possibilities of living in a new way and of interacting, dancing, and playing with the world oriented in discovery, play, and creativity. When these two substances are alchemically balanced and mixed, we can rest, explore, take risks, and participate in the bounty of this life. We don't need to hold back, overly protect ourselves, or hide from life. An accommodating holding environment provides the soil in which a baby's brain, heart, and nervous system can differentiate, grow, and come alive. It also provides the earthy and empathetic landscape in which we as adults can open and sink into the imaginative field of not knowing, where we are able to listen, feel, sense, and envision life in a new way. What a miracle. Real magic.

In addition to honoring the interpersonal aspect of holding, we need to examine the transpersonal dimension. From this perspective, our nature as open awareness might be conceived of as "the ultimate holding environment."[3] By "open awareness," I'm referring to a meditative experience of attunement to the space or ground in which all thoughts, feelings, and sensations arise and pass—that warm, spacious field in which our experience comes and goes. This "transpersonal" dimension of holding points to something beyond our biographical history to the open ground of unconditioned awareness, in which the entirety of our experience arises, dances for a short while, and then dissolves. This field of awareness holds whatever appears, without being tainted by it and without the brilliance or mirroring capacity of the field ever being affected. It is a clear, reflecting field in which thoughts, feelings, and emotions circle, spiral, and play as they unveil their qualities. We come to discover the nature and experience of this transpersonal holding through spiritual practices such as prayer, meditation, inquiry, ritual, creativity, and silence (or spontaneously without any effort), whereas interpersonal holding reveals itself in relationship with another person or figure (real or imaginal). Training ourselves to access, become familiar with, and relax into our true nature reveals the deeper dimensions of contact and space, where we come to the embodied realization that we are always, already being held by something infinite and vast. Although psychotherapeutic approaches have revealed the interpersonal nature of holding, the contemplative traditions provide the portal into this larger, already-existing dimension of experience.

Although as an infant we depended upon another to provide a holding environment for us, from a spiritual perspective we might imagine it as wired into the human person innately or organically, not as something acquired throughout our lives. In this sense, it is not dependent upon the empathic, skillful attunement of caregivers and key attachment figures, which many (most) of us were not fortunate enough to encounter, at least on a consistent basis. From this more contemplative view, our inner experience is made of primordial space—open, luminous, and inseparable from awareness itself. Every feeling, memory, image, emotion, sensation, and thought is crafted of strands of awareness. In other words, a holding environment is not built around us or created by way of relationship and external circumstances but is already present as an essential, unmanufactured aspect of our very own nature. The essential qualities of contact and space that cause a little nervous system to grow, unfold, and differentiate are the same substances that keep the stars from falling out of the sky and the life force moving in and out of our lungs, providing the foundation for healing, emotional maturity, and grounded spiritual discovery. This already-existing holding environment, seeded with the right alchemical mixture of attuned contact and primordial space, can take some practice to discover and even more practice and experience to get used to. Some of the meditatively oriented wisdom traditions (e.g., Mahamudra and Dzogchen in Tibetan Buddhism) offer teachings and practices to "point out" this essential nature and to help us to familiarize ourselves with it in our immediate experience. Even if we've touched into this reality by way of a temporary or "peak" experience, it can take some time to get used to because it can turn our ordinary, fixated perception upside down (and inside out).

We must each navigate these waters for ourselves and find the right balance and mixture of these two substances to achieve the ideal results. Too much contact and not enough space results in our being smothered and shut down, and our natural creativity and curiosity are dampened and eroded. Too much space and not enough contact, however, does not provide the rich relational field in which we feel seen, heard, and felt in a way that supports the (safe enough) exploration of new territory. If we reflect on our experience as children in our families of origin or as parents (to human or animal children), or even on our close, personal relationships, we might get a sense of how this balance between contact and space plays out in our lives. In this way, "contact" and "space" are alchemical substances, knitted together in the precise way that (ideally, of course) provides the optimal amount of provocative experience for us to develop and grow, challenging outmoded ways of organizing our perception, while not pushing us too far and too fast so that we become overwhelmed and experience unworkable levels of anxiety, fragmentation, and trauma.

Before we dive further into the experience of holding and being held, and the vast implications these ideas have for our larger theme of befriending difficult experience so we can heal, it might be helpful to explore why we don't just naturally "feel held" in the first place. In our early development, most of us did not have an adequate holding environment that offered an ideal or good-enough amount of contact and space or the empathic attunement required for us to trust in our experience as it is—a deep, inner knowing we are in fact worthy of holding. This (unfortunate) reality brings us into the area of neuroplasticity and the rewiring of the brain. Related to neuroplasticity is what attachment researchers refer to as "earned security," a dynamic process in which, over time, we can transform the effects of an early environment of insecure attachment (i.e., where contact or space was missing or not properly alchemically "mixed") to that of security. Only through befriending ourselves at the deepest levels will we be able to catalyze the transformative effects of neuroplasticity and bring about the earned security that will allow us to participate fully in our lives in a flexible, open, spontaneous, and creative way.

NEW PATHWAYS OF EXPERIENCE

We hear a lot these days—in the realms where spirituality, contemplative practice, and empirical science intersect (something not possible even fifty years ago)—about the phenomenon neuroscientists refer to as *neuroplasticity*, the innate capacity of the brain to rewire itself, for new experiential pathways to be embedded in the nervous system. Despite their discoveries of neuroplasticity at a theoretical level, it is important not to assume that it will *automatically* occur, outside of any effort from us. It takes practice to re-encode circuitry once organized by shame and dissociation, replacing habitual patterning of self-aggression and self-abandonment with empathy, attunement, and compassion. Yes, the brain is open and flexible and ready to embody new organization, but from a more poetic point of view, we must work together with the nervous system, befriend it as an ally and kindred traveler, and meet its receptivity with our own energy, intention, and experimentation.

The reality is that for many of us, this ideal neural foundation was not available as our brains and nervous systems were developing. For whatever reason, there was not an adequate holding environment to reflect back the authenticity and validity of our early emotional experience. As a result, we were not able to *feel felt.* We sensed the missing empathy at a deep and penetrating level and placed the blame for this lack of connection inside ourselves.[4] Because it was too unsafe to locate the failure outside us in the limitations of our caregivers, we took it on as clear evidence of our own core unlovability. As painful as this was, it was less disruptive than having to admit the truth that our parents were not (consistently) who we needed them to be—safe, interested, caring, and capable of truly seeing, validating, and honoring the integrity and uniqueness of our developing sense of self. This internalization of empathic failure—where we took the blame for the lack of connection, affection, and mirroring in our early attachment relationships—formed the foundation for the later (and often crushing) experience of low self-esteem so many of us deal with, a fundamental sense of unworthiness and feeling that there is something wrong with us at the most basic level.

Intellectual understanding, although vital, is not enough to catalyze neuroplasticity and to replace the perceptual grooves deepened over many years and decades. In addition to increased insight and awareness, it takes *action* in the moment, new here-and-now behavioral responses to the eruption of dysregulating thoughts and feelings, over time, for the nervous system to reorganize and for us to be able to reauthor a new, more nuanced, more complex, real-time, integrated narrative about who we are. We can't just *think* our way into the realities of neuroplasticity, lasting change, and transformation but must bring together cognitive, emotional, *and* behavioral ways of working to mine the reorganizing potential of the brain.

When in a moment of activation, or being triggered—for example, when someone doesn't respond in the way we'd like, criticizes or ignores us, or doesn't see us the way we long to be seen—instead of engaging in self-destructive behavior; automatically characterizing their response as clear evidence of our unworthiness; and falling down the rabbit hole of shame, blame, and self-attack, we are invited to slow down. When we can recognize what we are caught up in, we naturally cut the momentum of self-abandonment as we realize some old pain has been activated, and we have a choice to make. We can follow the thoughts and feelings down the familiar groove of denial, dissociation, or acting out, or we can choose a new way, bringing curiosity, presence, and compassion to the charged thoughts and body-based feelings. When we engage these latter pathways, it is then possible for us to perceive the activation not as an enemy coming from the outside to harm us but as an emissary of new life, ally of meaning and depth, and ambassador of neuroplasticity.

Of course, all this is much easier said than done, especially in a moment of activation and emotional overwhelm, but the point is that it is possible, *slowly, over time*—when we train ourselves in mindful self-reflection—to choose a new direction and to replace the habitual pathways of self-abandonment, shame, and self-aggression with the slower circuitry of empathy, attunement, and self-compassion.

Despite how hopeless it can feel in a particularly difficult moment, the good news is that you can begin *right now*, no matter what is going on in your life or how lost you believe you are. In fact, the *only* moment you can engage this work is *right now*. From this perspective, there is no work at a later time, no future moment when you can encode new circuitry and make a different choice. Instead of urgently scrambling for relief, falling into the ancient pathways of denial on the one hand, or seeking to immediately discharge the intensity on the other, you can practice becoming curious about the unique ways you become activated in relationship. You can train yourself to enter into communion with the burning, charged, claustrophobic, alive world of feeling. And in tending to and metabolization of that which seemed unmanageable at an earlier time, you can take advantage of the realities of neuro-plasticity and change the course of your life. Not all at once, over a powerful weekend, or by way of five simple steps, but slowly, moment by moment, in ways embodied and unique for you, into eternity. This work can take place only in the alchemical *vas* of your own immediate experience.

When you feel overwhelmed, caught in an avalanche of hot and sticky emotion, spiraling in repetitive thoughts and feeling the urge toward unhealthy or addictive behavior, slow way down. Ground your-self in your body and in the earth. Hold yourself. Allow yourself to be held by something greater—God, spirit, Source, an animal friend, a wise inner helper, an ally, a mountain, an ocean, or a star. Remember that you have what it takes to start right now, in *this* moment, to estab-lish a new pathway, to chart a new course, and to allow the miraculous implications of neuroplasticity to wash through you. When you hold yourself and your experience in a new way, meeting it with curiosity, slowness, space, and warmth—*even for only one second*—you light up the pathways within you and invite the revolutionary potentials of the brain, nervous system, and heart to encode new circuitry.

SAFETY AND STEPPING INTO NEW TERRITORY

As little ones, we were wired to conclude that "I *feel* bad" equaled "I *am* bad."[5] Neurobiologically, we were not capable of discerning between *feeling* and *being*, a developmental achievement that requires matura-tion over the course of a lifetime. We all know what it is like to identify with the passing presentation of thoughts, feelings, and emotions and then fuse with them, drown in them, or become flooded by them, losing contact altogether with who and what we are—the awareness that per-ceives them. This identification with open, spacious awareness is one of the great fruits of meditation. Although the original confusion was the perceptual reality of little ones in their families of origin, as adults we're in possession of capacities not available to us in earlier times. As we cultivate these soul faculties through meditation, therapeutic and relational work and experience with others, and our own unique inquiry in which we step back and reflect upon our experience with curiosity, spaciousness, and compassion, we can discover whether this conclusion is in fact accurate—that "I *feel* bad" equals "I *am* bad"— or whether it is ripe for revisioning. The implications of this sort of reorganization are vast because they filter down from our brains and nervous system into the cells of our hearts and into and through the relational field, affecting not only the dance with the external beloved, in all of his or her forms, but with the forgotten internal beloved, those lost soul parts and pieces of ourselves who long to know us once again.

This dissociative activity—disowning aspects of our lived experience to protect ourselves from states of unbearable feeling—was *not* unenlightened or pathological but profoundly skillful given the capacities we had at the time. It represented the most effective way we knew to care for ourselves and prevent overwhelming anxiety from rippling through our nervous systems, sending us outside our "window of tolerance" and into sympathetic flight-or-flight arousal or shutting us down into flattened states of immobilization.[6] The window of tolerance, the way I am using the term, refers to the unique balance of challenging experience that is provocative but not overwhelming, when we're in conscious relationship with the raw materials required for transformation but not to a degree in which we become anxious, fragmented, or traumatized so that we shut down. As we come to see the ways our adaptive strategies have served to protect us, we can remove the shame from their appearance in our lives and instead use their manifestations as fuel for deeper inquiry. "Ah, it's you again. Shame. Rage. Nausea. Tears. Looping thoughts that something is wrong with me. I know you. Please, come in for tea. I can't promise I will like or accept you just yet, but I will offer you a place at the table, in front of the fire, where we can speak with one another and establish a new relationship." This ability to distance ourselves from potentially crushing psychic states kept us from disintegrating into a fragmentation from which we might not have been able to recover. Although these deeply embedded responses might not be *current* expressions of the deepest wisdom within us, they served (and in some cases *continue* to serve) an incredibly important function and in this way might be viewed as early, partially developed forms of self-compassion. The point here is not to overly venerate the strategies but to remove the shame from them so that they can be seen and engaged more clearly in the here and now and updated to reflect current capacities and goals.

Although these decades-old ways of responding to agonizing emotional and somatic (i.e., body-based) experience was adaptive and played an essential role in self-protection, for many they are no longer serving a life of freedom, spontaneity, and aliveness. We long for something beyond mere protection and certainty, and although it is terrifying to step into a new world, for many it feels as if there is just no other choice. We know the consequences of standing on the sidelines and watching life go by, overprotecting ourselves, living at a distance from our openness and creativity, and not fully honoring what we know is most true. Although there might be some safety in this orientation, the result is that we do not feel alive; to a greater or lesser degree, we might feel frozen, flat, and bereft of meaning. And in this we come to the painful, yet empowering realization that we are not willing to trade authenticity and aliveness for security any longer. Although it might have been worth it—and even necessary—at an earlier time, it no longer is.

The realities of illuminating and transforming the dynamics involved in this trade-off—how it plays out in our relationships and the ways we have come to perceive ourselves, others, and the world—is a unique journey for each of us. Some are able to untangle the web in a way that feels natural and flowing, without a lot of upheaval and without the triggering of too much trauma from emotional wounding. I must confess that this outcome seems to represent the minority of people who engage this path, at least in my experience. For many—especially for those with early environments of attachment insecurity and some degree of developmental trauma (i.e., many of us)—it is important that we honor the realities of where we've come from to where we are. Though some will argue the possibility, we cannot simply make a choice one day to "get over it," tear down the entirety of our defensive organization, and replace it with wise, compassionate attunement. We must go slowly and respect the timeline written in the soul (and nervous system), go at a pace that honors our current situation, and remember there is no urgency on the path of healing. Yes, we must push ourselves a bit, or we will not be able to break through the momentum of habitual consciousness accumulated over a lifetime (or generations), but not so much or so fast that we overwhelm or retraumatize ourselves, which only keeps the current neural pathways in place and even strengthens patterns of misattunement. Learning to surf the edges of our window of tolerance is a capacity worthwhile to cultivate, but we must also develop the wisdom to discern when we are going too quickly and merely reenacting earlier patterns of self-aggression. And in this recognition, with no shame and no blame, shift the way we work, rest, and then try again at another time.

REACTIVITY AND THE ANCIENT PATHWAYS

In a moment of activation—when we are triggered and caught in the grip of a limiting belief, challenging emotion, disturbing body-based sensation, or overwhelming urge to act in an unhealthy way—the ancient pathways of fight, flight, and freeze appear, providing doorways out of the intensity as quickly and efficiently as possible. Although these primary responses are usually viewed as relatively unconscious, instinctual states of reactivity, I find it empowering and imaginally activating to conceive of them as "pathways" that we can navigate with some (newly discovered) choice, as forks in the road, trails to pursue, and portals to explore, providing relevant data and experience. Although each has served an important adaptive function in protecting us from overwhelming anxiety, their automatic engagement might not be serving our deepest longing for a life of freedom and spontaneity. The goal is not to "get rid" of these responses, for that would not be possible or desirable, but to act in a more creative, more intelligent, and kinder way. It is unrealistic and even aggressive to believe we will overcome hundreds of thousands of years of evolution by learning some psychological or meditative techniques. But that's okay, we need not eliminate these wired-in strategies but only flood them with curiosity, awareness, and compassion. As I continue to elaborate throughout the book, the goal is always more *consciousness*, forming the basis from which wiser and more skillful responses flow.

On one end of the spectrum we deny or repress unwanted experience in an attempt to locate it outside awareness, where we can be free of its intensity and perceived threat. Of course, there are times when this strategy is appropriate and effective, but when it comes to healing and transforming the deeper layers, when we are not in immediate danger or on the brink of some inner catastrophe, we want to illuminate what we're doing and clarify our intentions. The acts of repression and denial correspond to the "flight" reaction, in which we flee or distance ourselves from our immediate here-and-now experience in the hope of avoiding the energetic disturbance often lurking just under the surface. In this family of strategies we find a lot of our addictive behavior, such as unhealthy drinking, eating, shopping, sexuality, drug use, and media bingeing. Although movement away from ourselves can be *temporarily* effective and certainly has its place, in the long run it is usually not the wisest, most skillful, or most compassionate choice. If we do not relate with our experience consciously and directly, it remains in the shadow, where it can be worked with only by way of its unconscious manifestations, which usually come in less-than-desirable ways. Manifestations such as emotional outbursts, saying things we later regret, addictions, existential flatness or meaninglessness, chronic anxiety and depression, and even aggression and violence can be the result of not tending to important feelings and emotions with care.

In the language of attachment theorists, the developmental psychologists who explore how we bond as infants with critical figures around us (or as adults in romantic and other relationships), flight or denial-based responses correspond loosely with *avoidance,* when we close down and *deactivate* the attachment system in hope that doing so will soothe the fire and bring us back into a state of homeostasis. If we can effectively purge the difficult thought, feeling, or sensation from our experience, we think we can then avoid its untoward effects, which usually involve a deeper confrontation with our own vulnerability and sensitivity.

On the other end of the spectrum is the "fight" response, which does not so much deny, numb, or repress what we're experiencing but generates a more active engagement to seek discharge from the underlying anxiety through behavior we hope will get us out of overwhelm and back to safe ground. Colloquially referred to as "acting out," this strategy includes compulsive activity in which we urgently scramble to get our needs met in less than healthy ways: blaming or attacking others, pushing them away and then immediately pulling them back, panicking and texting incessantly when the other does not immediately return our call, and more generally moving out into the environment or toward another for hopes of regulation. We are caught up and tangled in the thoughts and feelings, and we need release, spinning outward in hopes of soothing the intensity.

With respect to the specific attachment response most native to us, we might equate the fight reaction to *anxious* attachment, in which we *hyperactivate* the attachment system, moving anxiously toward the other in the hope they will provide the regulation we need to come back online and into a manageable state. We spin toward the other to meet our needs and confirm that everything is okay, so they see us in the way we need to be seen and somehow remove us from what appears to be impending abandonment and overwhelm. We are unable to regulate ourselves and thus begin the journey outward, marching toward another person to somehow help us to discharge or soothe the underlying anxiety and uncertainty.

It's important to note that there are healthy and unhealthy ways of reaching out to another in times of need to help us coregulate difficult and threatening emotional states. In fact, the capacity to turn to another in times of distress is one of the critical aspects of secure attachment, as I noted earlier, and an expression of the sacredness and preciousness of our human experience. It's important to note that there is a healthy or adaptive turning toward another for help and an unhealthy, addictive, or avoidant way that often ends in further suffering and struggle, for us and for them, and tends to serve those older pathways of misattuned self-abandonment, shame, and blame. To discern between these, in ways that will be unique for each of us, is one of the critical tasks we must encounter and work through on any path of deep healing and transformation.

Finally, in the "freeze" response, we become flooded by our immediate experience to such a degree that the only way we can effectively handle what has become unbearable is to shut down. It has gotten to the point that we cannot successfully repress the overwhelming thoughts and feelings or move effectively out into the world for help. This is a response some of us learned as children in environments of consistent trauma and empathic failure, where we were not able to flee or fight, and the only option was to unplug from conscious engagement by way of dissociation. Loosely speaking, we could equate this strategy with *disorganized* attachment, usually associated with trauma, neglect, and abuse. The freeze response is often likened to the adaptive strategy we see in animals in which they "play dead" in the face of impending attack by a predator in hopes that the aggressor will bypass them. We can recognize a freeze response when we find ourselves a bit checked out, not fully there, out of touch with our experience and surroundings, and disconnected from our bodies. We can't really feel anything (other than a vague sense of flatness or helplessness); we're numb, blurry, and scattered, unsure of what we're thinking. It's as if our thoughts and emotions are happening not *in* us, but somehow just *outside* us. We can't quite relate to our experience because we're not fully there as the experience-er. It's as if we're looking down upon it from some other place. We can't really fight or flee. Somehow neither of these are options, even if we determine that one or the other would be an effective response to the situation. We just can't do it.

These three evolutionary strategies are wired into the brain as part of all human beings. Their constellation in a moment of emotional activation is not evidence that we have failed, are "unspiritual," or have done something wrong but that we have a tender, beating heart and open, sensitive, functioning nervous system. From this perspective, even these pathways are expressions of the sacred, of something pure and even holy. It is an act of great self-compassion to slow down and begin to observe these hardwired responses to stress and emotional activation, not so that we can attack, shame, or judge ourselves as they inevitably arise but so that we can bring increasing awareness and kindness to ourselves and slowly begin to chart a new course.

By familiarizing ourselves with these instinctual ways of responding to difficult and challenging experience, we build a foundation for a new way to befriend ourselves and choose differently in a moment when we are triggered. Instead of falling down a rabbit hole and following the habitual reactive grooves of shame, blame, and self-attack, we slow down, become curious, and meet ourselves afresh. Seeing clearly how and in what specific situations we engage the pathways of fight, flight, and freeze allows us to "hold" our experience in a new way. Remember that the holding we are speaking about spans intrapsychic (personal), relational, and spiritual domains. Personally, we can learn to hold parts of ourselves and our experience in a new way and at other times receive this holding from another. The more spiritual, or transpersonal aspect of holding, however, involves an experiential realization (which tends to deepen over time) that a dimension of our experience is untouched by difficult experience, was never harmed by what happened to us in the past, and was always "securely attached" in our relationship with God or the Divine or the Soul or Spirit. This realization can be incredibly healing and transformative because it brings alive the direct awareness that we need not change our past to heal, to awaken, or to transform at the deepest levels.

ILLUMINATING OUR PREFERRED STRATEGY

As part of your inquiry, it can be helpful to discover which of the strategies you most naturally turn to in the face of challenging experience. When you are triggered, what is your first line of defense, the most familiar pathway of reaction, the one that hardly takes any effort at all but seems to just be waiting there to greet you? For example, let's say a new partner promises to text you at a certain time and doesn't, your boss critiques your contribution to a project, or someone implies that you are horribly unspiritual or ignorant. The important point is to investigate what, *specifically for you*, brings about that hooked quality, in which the situation gets hot, claustrophobic, and sticky; in which you feel trapped, as if you're starting to slide down a hole or rocket out of your body; and in which you feel the rage, the shame, the irritation, the embarrassment, the panic. How do you respond? What is that automatic, knee-jerk, in-the-moment reaction most native to you—the one with the goal of removing you from the underlying vulnerability and impending sense of overwhelm as quickly as possible?

The invitation is to begin to familiarize yourself with these dynamics *in the moment*, not in order to shame, judge, or beat yourself up for not staying calm and holding it all together *but so that you can begin to care for yourself in a new way* oriented in insight, empathy, and compassion. Over time, the goal is not to have to follow the pathways of misattunement, aggression, and abandonment but to slowly begin to become more flexible, wise, and skillful in the ways you respond during times of activation. Remember, this work can only be done in the immediate moment. Just *this* moment. And *this* one. Don't overwhelm yourself by contemplating how you will do with dozens of future moments—"I'll never be able to do that"—and other predictions. *None of us* can care for or tend a future moment. Remove that pressure and burden from yourself. Be kind and stay close to yourself, right here, right now. Can you turn to yourself in *this* moment?

Contrary to what we often believe in a moment of being triggered, the mere appearance of these hooks is not evidence that something has gone wrong, that we have fallen short, that we are bad people or neurotic or have lost our way. Remember that these strategies arose as our best ways to care for ourselves at an earlier time when we did not have the capacities to stay with, metabolize, and integrate anxiety and other challenging emotional states. But if you have made it this far in the book, you are ready and able to take that next step into a new world.

To fight, flee, or freeze is not an error, mistake, or sign of failure but evidence of a certain kind of intelligence, creativity, and even grace. No, those actions might not represent the most up-to-date, wise, and skillful response, but they need not be rejected or judged wholesale because to do so has a way of keeping them alive and reinforcing their prominence in our experience. Remember, the primary invitation is not to rejection, purging, or deleting parts of ourselves but to expanding consciousness of what is happening, for it is from that increased awareness that we can choose a new way.

Although these strategies served a lifesaving function at one point in your life, you might come to discover that the mere repetition of these behaviors are no longer necessary in all situations and in many ways are interfering with a life of freedom, spontaneity, and flow. Now you have other capacities that you can rely on in moments when you truly need yourself more than ever. Although you might never completely step outside your neurobiological wiring, you can lean on your familiar strategies in those moments that you need them and implement other ways of being when the original strategies are not necessary.

INTO THE SACRED MIDDLE

Within the sacred middle, that alive territory in-between the conditioned reactivity of flight-flight-freeze, we are invited, slowly at first, into an experiment in self-care. For just one or two seconds at a time, we can begin to replace the old pathways with something fresh, to overwrite the conditioned circuitry of self-abandonment with the new wiring of empathy, mindfulness, and lovingkindness. Here, we can enter a profound intimacy with our experience while at the same time not fusing with it, falling in, and becoming flooded by it. Close, but not so close we lose perspective. Intimate, but not so intimate we become lost in our experience and identify with it as who we are in an absolute sense. Navigating and dancing in this unfamiliar middle territory is something we can all experiment with and come to know experientially at a pace that is right for us, based on our own direct experience, and rooted in deeper levels of curiosity and compassion.

As we continue to explore between the extremes of fusion (unhealthy merging) and repression (denying unwanted experience) and stay open and curious in the unresolvable nature of the center, we naturally generate rest and creativity, and a new freedom dawns—alive, unprecedented, and filled with new vision. Just so we're clear, when I speak about "fusion," I am referring to the experience of losing touch with ourselves and our own integrity and "blending" with another in an unhealthy way. To start to see the specific ways we respond in a moment of activation is essential on the path of healing, though it is not easy.

It can be humbling to discover just how many of our go-to, habitual, addictive behaviors and ways of being are organized around getting us out of feelings we do not want to feel, in the attempt to protect us from raw, tender vulnerability at the core.

One reason some of us tend toward fusion is that it was once an adaptive strategy, an effective (and potentially lifesaving) way to keep us out of some vulnerable, unworkable anxiety and other emotional material we did not have the capacity to metabolize. These ways of responding to overwhelming experience do not often yield completely to increased knowledge and awareness but require cultivating the capacity and tolerance to slowly, bit by bit, contain, hold, and integrate the feeling states that historically (and currently) we'll do just about anything to avoid.

Unless we grew up around enlightened parents, teachers, and authority figures, none of us was trained in becoming familiar with and navigating this middle area, and we do not have psychological, emotional, somatic, or neurobiological reference points for it. To generate a new way of organization requires a complete retraining of the nervous system and emotional, physical, mental, and spiritual bodies; it's as if we were starting afresh as total beginners. We can honor this reality and not shame ourselves for not being able to "do it right" when we inevitably fall apart and do not heal ourselves as quickly as we were hoping. There is no urgency on this path, and it unfolds according to its own timeline.

It's important to remember that ideas such as the "middle place" are images, meant to be evocative and provocative, to stimulate feeling, imagination, creative thinking, and intuition for us to work with and enter into relationship with, not reified "places" that exist in some objective sense. We need not "find" some middle place in a literal way in order to engage this process. We will not likely discover the "middle place" by way of empirical investigation but imaginatively, phenomenologically, and experientially within the fire of our direct, embodied experience. This "middle place," which we must discover for ourselves, reveals an alive dimension of experience. In the middle, in the center, we are always, already held; life itself is holding us. From this perspective, holding is not something that one day will happen *to us*, but something we realize is always occurring. Training ourselves to recognize this middle territory helps us to discover experientially that no matter what is happening in our lives, we are held by something greater than ourselves, even our most challenging experience is workable, and intelligence underlies it. It is not an error or mistake but an instinctual expression of a natural urge toward integration and wholeness.

SANCTUARY FOR THE UNWANTED

As a way of investigating this territory for yourself, you might ask: What feeling state will I do just about anything to avoid? What is the one emotion or inner experience, more than any other, I am determined to stay out of at all costs? Sadness? Grief? Rage? Shame? Uncertainty? Joy? Rest? Peace? Remember, it's not only the so-called negative emotions we avoid but also "positive" ones that, when activated, can generate anxiety or resistance within us. To what degree are you able and willing to let yourself *be* angry or sad or confused or ashamed without having to do anything about it? Or to let yourself enter a state of deep rest, or to feel causeless joy?

What would it be like, for just this one moment, to turn *toward* that feeling with curiosity, acceptance, and even kindness? To befriend your experience in a new way and not fall into the ancient pathways of fight, flight, or freeze? Remember, the experiment is always conducted in *this* moment, not a future moment. You *cannot* tend to your future experience, and attempting to do so is overwhelming for any of us—a future moment's pain, confusion, or struggle is not possible to work with. Future experience cannot be found in the vessel. But what about *this* moment's thoughts, images, urges, and feelings?

Just take a few minutes and begin to connect with those thoughts, feelings, and sensations you have tended to avoid; the ones that if and when they begin to arise, from which you act quickly to disconnect. This can be subtle. As you start to cultivate some awareness of specifically what this looks like for you, *slowly* start to invite that feeling-based material in so you can touch it, hold it, and embrace its qualities and textures for only one second at a time.

Begin to train yourself, with an outpouring of self-compassion, to build the neural foundation and resources that for many of us were just not available from the earliest times of our development. Push yourself just a bit, but not so far that you begin to spiral outside your window of tolerance. Familiarize yourself with what it would be like to surf the edges of that window, which for most requires short and frequent periods of practice.

Resist the natural temptation to "stay" for hours and days, determined to do whatever it takes to root it all out and fix, cure, or "heal" yourself. For this latter approach is usually an enactment of the way our families of origin met our emotional experience as little ones. It is rarely an expression of self-compassion but usually an act of self-abandonment and self-aggression that only reinforces the neural patterning that the feeling is a "problem" we must "deal with"; that is, repress, purge, or act out (sometimes disguised in more spiritual-sounding language as "heal" or "transcend").

In addition to this mindfulness-based approach, in a more imaginative way, we can discover the image hidden within the emotion—locate the "figure" who dwells inside the feeling and enter into dialogue with this one.[7] Perhaps a wise old woman awaits you, or a scared little boy, a tree, quicksand, a being of light, a darkened forest, or a black hole.

Allow this one safe passage in your inner awareness. You need not "see" the image visually (this is not a native way of perceiving for many of us) but sense it in your own way. Ask why she has come, what he needs, what message they have for you, and where it is pointing you.

Don't engage only with your mind, but open yourself to the emotion and feel what is evoked. Yes, pay attention to the thoughts and beliefs, but often just underneath the conceptual spin is important information at the level of feeling. For when all is said and done, perhaps a turning of the heart, not mere insight or even increased awareness (which, of course, are also critical), will heal the wounds of a lifetime. For some, personifying the feeling and mood can help to bring intimacy with our experience more naturally than attempting to open our hearts to an abstract or clinical notion such as rage, shame, or depression. But, as Jung suggests, if we find the image or the figure within the core of the emotion, we can open a portal into deeper engagement. In this sense, the underlying image is the master key, even more primary than the thoughts, feelings, moods, and impulses that dance on the surface of conscious awareness. This discovery of the primacy of the image, brought into the contemporary world by Jung (and enlarged by others), forms the basis of an imaginal psychology, an approach to the soul oriented in tending to images. We can see this most vividly, for example, in those few moments when we awaken in the morning and the images from the dreamworld are still lingering in our awareness.

There is a deeply rooted belief that the best way to care for ourselves is to *turn away* from feeling, from this tender sensitivity, and from what is happening in our bodies during times of activation. This is a belief we inherited from our personal, cultural, and archetypal histories, and we must discover for ourselves whether it is true, *now*. Ask yourself: Is it accurate that abandoning my vulnerability and falling into denial or acting out is truly providing the care I most long for in a moment of being triggered into pain or struggle? Although we might *feel* like what we most need is protection, numbing, and relief, our own presence, love, and holding meet the deepest longing in our hearts. By "holding" our experience in a new way, meeting it with curiosity and kindness—while simultaneously opening to the possibility that we are being "held" by something greater than ourselves—we begin to encode new pathways that allow us to unearth the wisdom and creativity in even our most challenging circumstances. We cannot take anyone's word for this, though, and must plumb the depths of our own experience to find the unique truths about this for ourselves.

After we begin to see more clearly what is going on and the nature of our conditioned responses, we are then able to map a new way, to catch these strategies as they emerge in a constellated here-and-now moment and replace them, over time, with responses oriented in mindfulness, acceptance, and self-compassion. Cultivating loving attention to the ways we've come to organize our experience and bringing new levels of awareness and kindness to ourselves are foundational and powerful expressions of this theme of "holding." To truly hold our experience, we must first contact it in a curious, interested, caring, and even intimate way, replacing the old way of self-abandonment in times of stress and activation with that of empathy and warmth.

HARBINGERS OF INTEGRATION

As a way to cultivate this curious attention and begin to hold your experience in a new way, I want to share an inquiry in which you can engage in a moment of activation, when you are upset, stressed, or thrown off center. Anytime you wish to come closer to yourself, to enter into relationship with the soul parts and pieces with which you sense you might have lost contact, or anytime you feel drawn to provide a deeper level of warmth, attention, and kindness to your experience, I invite you to try this inquiry. Although it can be helpful to contemplate the idea of holding and meeting our experience in a theoretical way, it all comes alive when we find ourselves in the midst of cascading thoughts and feelings that seem to be happening to us from the outside, coming of their own accord, and threatening to take us down. The following is a short exercise or meditation you can do during these times. As soon as you realize you've been hooked or triggered, take a few deep breaths, recognize what has happened, and state a simple intention to become curious so as not to abandon yourself and fall down the rabbit hole into the habitual pathways. "This time, I will try something different."

When your emotional world is on fire, and you are cycling in the claustrophobia of ruminative thought, pause and return attention into your body. It only takes one moment to return to curious interest, shifting awareness out of the swirling narrative and into the life moving through you. With this act, you offer rest to the spinning thoughts, feelings, and bodily sensations and surround them with warmth. This is what allows relationship to take place, this field of safety and presence, where the entirety of what you are is welcome. Open to the possibility that the visitors—as they come in the form of ruminative thoughts, painful feelings, heat or cold, pressure in the body, or irresistible impulses—do so not to harm or take you down but to be allowed home, to step into the relational field with you and release their message.

Drop underneath the compelling story line and into the alive world of feeling, sensation, and image. You can return to the story, characters, plot, drama, and climax at a later moment after the activation has been soothed with the cooling rains of loving awareness. From that more grounded, earthy place, you will be better able to access, articulate, and make sense of what happened, reauthoring the story in more integrated and cohesive and less shadowy ways.

After you locate the intensity within the emotional or physical body, practice breathing *into* or *with* it. Instead of falling into one of the old strategies of repression or acting out, slow down and cut into the sense of urgency with breath and with the earth as your witness.

With your hand on your heart, renew your vow to no longer abandon yourself. Even if for only one or two seconds, use your awareness and the warmth of your presence to infuse what is arising with curiosity, empathy, and kindness for the journey you've been on. Slow down the momentum of billions of moments of self-aggression, and lay down a new pathway.

It all starts with the capacity and the willingness to recognize that we've been triggered—that the visitors have arrived, the figures of the psyche who've been trying to reach us for so long, not as obstacles for us to overcome but as orphaned parts of ourselves who only long to be allowed back home. Instead of meeting with shame, judgment, and blame the discovery that we have been hooked, we might cultivate our gratitude for the gift of awareness and see if we must act urgently to protect ourselves from the life surging within us. This momentary awareness alone is a true miracle.

Each of us must experiment for ourselves and see what is most true *now*, not what was true in the past or what our parents, teachers, therapists, family, or friends said was true. Each of us must set this and every book aside for a moment and finally turn toward ourselves in a moment of activation, see within, and provide sanctuary for the pounding in the heart, shakiness in the belly, and hopelessness in the throat. We infuse this surging life with presence, care, mercy, and compassion. "No, this time I will not turn away. I will not leave myself in this moment and spin out into shame, blame, judgment, and rejection. Just *this* time, I will stay close. And listen. Feel. And see."

This pause is a threshold to a new world where we are standing on a precipice with a cliff below and the stars above, where we are invited to travel inside that alive, creative, alchemical middle place in which new circuitry can take birth and bloom. It is an act of profound kindness to provide safe passage for the visiting feelings, emotions, and sensations as they wash through us, conveying significant information for the journey ahead. Yes, we might feel as if we need to numb ourselves or quickly seek relief, but this is the old groove laid down in personal and collective networks for billions of moments and kept alive each time we turn away. Through compassionate presence and the warmth of mindful awareness, we offer a home for these ancient companions where they can rest, be cared for and listened to, and then continue along their way.

You are okay. Go slow. There is no urgency now. Stay with the sensations as they rise and fall in your belly and your heart. For just a second or two at first, just see.

Waves are washing in, yes, not as obstacles or enemies but as harbingers of integration, seeking to find their rightful place within your wild ecology. As you return, over and over again, into the aliveness of the somatic world, slowly the love will dissolve the tangles and the knots. And all that will remain is a luminous field of awareness, warmth, and creativity. For this is what you are.

Let us take a moment to rest and open to the notion that we are already being held by something vast. Take a few deep breaths, feel our feet on the ground, and realize that no matter what is happening in our lives, we and our experience are contained; without having to earn or deserve it, we are supported in ways we might not fully understand or be able to perceive at this time. I am not suggesting you believe this out of some expression of blind faith or just take my word for it, but just open to the possibility.

Over time, as our inquiry and experience deepen, we might discover an increasing trust in our ability to return to this ground in times of stress, confusion, and challenge, in which we can tap into resources previously unavailable. Through this practice, we begin to build a certain confidence that *whatever* comes in our lives (as inner experience), even if difficult and intense, is valid in some fundamental way and need not be rejected. But more than anything it is *workable*, and we need not abandon ourselves or our experience in times of activation.

3

SELF-COMPASSION AND CARING FOR OURSELVES IN A NEW WAY

IN THIS CHAPTER, WE WILL DEEPEN our exploration of what it might look and feel like to come closer to ourselves, to replace old, worn-out pathways of self-aggression and self-abandonment with kindness and true care. We continue to step into new territory at a pace that is provocative but not overwhelming, honoring the realities of where we are as well as our longing to reach into the depths. To do this, we must explore novel ways of tending to challenging experience and the potential meaning and purpose of even our most intense and disturbing thoughts and feelings, and with as much subtlety as possible, *how* we are thrown off-center. As always, the goal is not to "get rid of" experience we do not like, replacing it with more desirable states, but to increase our consciousness of what is happening in a moment of activation. From the ground of this enlarged consciousness, we become more flexible, skillful, and compassionate in our responses.

Jung discovered that our difficult experience constellated in clusters of energy that he called "complexes." These complexes arise from emotionally triggering life situations, and they organize around specific themes in our lives such as mother, father, money, sexuality, abandonment, and inferiority. They consist of psychically charged thoughts, feelings, images, and behaviors that have a way of taking over our ordinary awareness during times of stress and activation. Colloquially, we refer to this process as being "triggered," "hooked," or "activated," and for a few seconds or minutes (or hours) it can seem as if our "ordinary consciousness" has been usurped by some outside force. For example, we're in a conversation with someone and then suddenly out of nowhere we are flooded with a cascading waterfall of hot, sticky, claustrophobic thoughts and feelings, as if we're being pulled down into some sort of hole. Our perception is altered, our experience becomes inflamed, and we fall off-center. Later, we might even say, "Wow, what happened? That wasn't 'me'."

Although cultivating deeper layers of insight into precisely *how* we get caught in a complex, including tracing its origin throughout our personal history, can be helpful in depotentiating the energetic constellations, increasing our awareness is often not enough. This is a common realization I hope to invite in this book—the discovery that insight, however helpful and clarifying, is not usually enough to transform outmoded and tangled perceptions and ways of organizing experience. Although intellectual clarity is critical to unraveling our complexes, greater understanding tends to take us only so far. Even if we can bring new levels of perception to the nature of the complexes and the specific thoughts, feelings, and behaviors that constitute it, we've all had the experience of "knowing" what's going on but still not being able to "do" anything about it, especially in real time.

We can have a great deal of knowledge about these complexes, but in a moment of activation, all that knowing doesn't really seem to help that much as we find ourselves tangled in shame, rage, blame, and self-attack. From within the charged state, awareness is not always synonymous with the transformation of the painful thoughts and feelings, not to mention our unhealthy behaviors in response. In addition to cognitive insight and perspective, we must bring in the emotional body as well as new, skillful, in-the-moment behavioral changes and new ways of responding live and on the ground. This takes a lot of practice and the willingness to meet, tolerate, contain, and work through a variety of challenging, anxiety-based experiences.

Jung described the complexes as autonomous portions of the psyche behaving like independent beings, suggesting that they have a life of their own because they operate in large part outside our ordinary and conscious control.[1] Before we know it, they arrive into awareness and cloud perception, hooking us into all sorts of painful (yet familiar) ways of thinking, feeling, and acting. They have a way of commandeering ordinary consciousness, taking us over in a moment of activation, cutting through (and liquefying) even our most profound insights and realizations. Perhaps we thought of ourselves as nice, patient, open, content, peaceful, empathic, caring, nonjudgmental, independent, spiritually awake, compassionate, and emotionally healed. But when we are caught in the grip of a complex, these qualities are nowhere to be found. Instead, much to our surprise and consternation, their opposites are alive and spinning in our experience, coloring the lenses through which we see ourselves and others and how we navigate our close, personal relationships. As Jung provocatively noted, "Everyone knows nowadays that people 'have complexes.' What is not so well known, though far more important theoretically, is that complexes can *have us*."[2]

Sometimes all it takes is someone looking at us in a certain way or saying or doing something rather innocuous—not calling us when they said they would, not seeing us as we would like to be seen, misunderstanding or abandoning us in a moment when we need them, or offering a relatively reasonable critique of our work, speech, or appearance. As a network of feeling-toned associations, the complex gathers energy like a tornado as it twirls across the plains. In my experience, more important than deepening insight into these complexes is finding a way to bring compassion, kindness, and the transformative warmth of the heart to these clusters of energy. It seems that self-love truly is the medicine that has the power to melt the complex over time, not *instead of* increased awareness but in addition to it. Mere cognitive insight, although critical, is often not enough. A full-bodied response that touches each of the layers and dimensions of our experience seems to be required. More on this later in chapter 5.

The way we bring kindness to our experience and meet what is arising with compassion and warmth will look different for each of us; what opens the heart in a given moment is unique for each person. Taking a walk in nature, speaking with a friend, laying our hands on a part of the body that needs extra attention, speaking to an inner child, saying a prayer, and engaging in a healing visualization are examples of practices that work for some in different situations. The point here is that not merely an intellectual approach but a turning of the heart is required to untangle the complex from its historical associations. One without the other just does not seem to generate the requisite energy to overcome the built-up momentum.

THE TWO WINGS OF WISDOM AND COMPASSION

We find an analogous view in Tibetan Buddhism, for example, which says both wisdom *and* compassion are required to reach the deepest levels of realization. Where only one "wing" is present, the bird is unable to fly, or flies in a way that is disembodied and disconnected from its inherent wholeness. Even as we incorporate both, engaging in the work of increasing awareness *and* deepening compassion, we might never eradicate the complex, per se, or fully eliminate it from our experience. No matter how much inner work we do, there is no guarantee that the activation will not occur in a future moment. Fortunately, it is not necessary that we purge the charged thoughts and feelings and remove or delete them from our experience in some wholesale and "final" way; it is only necessary to bring more spaciousness and warmth to them when they inevitably appear. Paradoxically, the continued arising of the complex allows us to deepen in ways not possible if our triggers were removed completely. The triggers allow us to think certain thoughts, feel certain feelings, and sense certain bodily sensations that might not be available in an "uncharged" state. Opening to this possibility supports my primary thesis in this book: wisdom, guidance, mercy, and even a certain type of grace are available in the core of our most difficult experience. But cleansed perception as well as new levels of self-compassion are required to mine this gold.

Practitioners of certain alchemical and meditative traditions believe that our wounds contain information, and if we eliminate the hurt places, we will lose contact with the organic and inherent intelligence within them. Though our complexes might never be permanently removed, our relationships with them can change profoundly. Even though they might continue to arise, they do so within the context of enormous space. Although perhaps still frustrating and unideal, they are no longer able to throw us off-center in the same way and tend to dissolve in shorter and shorter amounts of time.

For example, a difficult conversation triggering cascading shame, rage, overwhelm, and abandonment that once took an hour (or more) to digest and metabolize might lose its charge in thirty minutes, or fifteen, or five. Eventually, in some situations, we might even notice that the activated material dissolves simultaneously with its arising because we are able to infuse immediate experience with new levels of curiosity, warmth, and awareness in real time (or close to it).

In certain meditative experience, although challenging thoughts, feelings, and sensations continue to emerge in moments of activation, they lose their charge almost immediately. The process of arising and dissolution coemerge, revealing not two processes but one. If we observe carefully, we might not be able to separate the arising-dissolving cycle.

This is something we can each experiment with, slowly, for a few seconds at a time, within the fire of our own direct experience. It can help to start with feelings and situations where there is a mild charge, and then to slow down and to begin to isolate the cycle in which we can sense directly the arising of emotion and how it stays for a short while and then dissolves back into the space from which it came. We sort of reverse-engineer the activation process, almost as if we were in slow motion, to familiarize ourselves with how the dance of emotion is at work within us. And most importantly, we can begin to discover in an experiential way whether there is suffering *inherent* in our emotional experience or to what degree it arises in the rejection of it—or from self-abandonment in moments of overwhelm and unexamined conclusions about what the mere appearance of certain feelings mean about us (e.g., that we've failed, that something is wrong with us, that we're unlovable, etc.).

In Vajrayana Buddhism, it is said that there is a particular quality of wisdom found in the core of specific difficult emotions, and the only way to mine that intelligence is through the direct apprehension and metabolization of the underlying energy. If we prematurely "go around" the emotion—repress it or act it out—or if we become flooded by or fused with it, we lose contact with that underlying wisdom at its core. Training ourselves to go into intense emotions; stay embodied with them; and infuse them with warmth, presence, and clear awareness is essential on the path of healing and is a theme I address throughout this book.

As we become more familiar with our complexes over time, although they might continue to appear in moments of dysregulation and stress, they become background to the foreground of spacious curiosity and awareness. There is plenty of room for the trigger to play and dance and express its qualities without our becoming flooded by it, on the one hand, or having to repress it, on the other. Because at the center of each of our personal complexes is an archetypal core; Jung believed

70

that we could never fully get rid of the complexes. Because they are not "ours" alone and emanate from the collective unconscious, arising out of psychic patterning we share with all other human beings, no matter how much we work on ourselves, the complexes never completely dissolve. But our relationships with them can transform immensely when we are able to make use of the energetic constellation to generate more insight, more consciousness, and more kindness for ourselves and others. In this way, *the complexes shift from being enemies to allies*, revealing themselves to be important friends and guides in our own healing.

An old Tibetan yogi once explained to me that like a bull raging in a wide-open meadow, the complex (or emotional activation) by its very nature will spin and twirl and emanate its chaotic energy, but it does so in a field of vast space. If that same bull releases its essence within a small, enclosed container (an inflexible heart and mind), it is likely to wreak havoc. It's similar to when a star explodes and nothing is nearby; the eruption occurs in pure silence. As with alchemists' quest to find the proper vessel in which to engage the work of transmutation, a spacious, flexible *vas* can provide the foundation required for the heated material to unravel, unwind, and reveal its golden nature. Within this more spacious context, although the trauma from the complex might be intense and even painful, we are not thrown off-center, or even if we are, we return. Over time and with practice, we can discover newfound flexibility in the ways we respond to emotional triggers and can make use of their provocative energy to deepen our inquiry, learn more about ourselves, and discover empathy and compassion for others caught in a similar situation.

INTO THE ALCHEMICAL MIDDLE

There is a creative and pregnant moment we can discover in-between our emotion erupting and our taking action in response. Training ourselves to recognize and explore this middle territory is an act of self-compassion that provides an incredible amount of information. In times when we are hooked in a torrent of limiting beliefs and overwhelming feelings, a doorway opens, and we see a fork in the road. In one direction, we follow the impulse to turn from the hot, sticky, claustrophobic material—by way of the previously discussed pathways of denial or acting out—or stay with the underlying energy and surround it with new levels of awareness, curiosity, and warmth. Within this charged middle territory, we can choose something different, establish a new pathway, encode new circuitry, and establish original behaviors oriented not in habitual reaction but in wise, empathic attunement. Familiarizing ourselves with this middle place—its qualities and felt sense—allows us to recognize the transformative nature of these moments, which catalyze the unfolding of neuroplasticity, establishing new networks of skillful response that over time reduce suffering and struggle for ourselves as well as others.

What we most need in these moments is to provide an inner sanctuary, or heart container, for the charged thoughts and feelings to be held, explored, and metabolized. When caught in habitual consciousness, we have no choice but to engage in familiar pathways of reactivity, as noted earlier, designed to remove us as quickly as possible from what appears as unworkable states of overwhelm and anxiety. It feels as if we *must* do *whatever* it takes to get back to center; otherwise, the consequences could be devastating as we tumble outside our window of tolerance into autonomic arousal, mobilizing fight-flight reactivity or immobilizing by way of dissociation and freeze, each of these ancient strategies, which emerged to protect us from full-scale psychic devastation.[3]

Although these approaches have served an important (even life-saving) function, the shadow side is that their effectiveness requires us to disown or disconnect from valid inner experience, splitting off from thoughts, emotions, and parts of ourselves seeking care and attention, with the goal of eradicating the unwanted material as quickly as possible. It just feels so urgent in the moment, as if some action must be taken immediately to avoid breaking apart or falling into some danger-ous, unworkable state.

This concern—which spans neurobiological, psychological, emo-tional, somatic (i.e., body-based), and even spiritual levels—was reasonable and accurate in earlier times when we did not have the devel-opmental capacities to stay with and metabolize intense feeling states. Our little brains and nervous systems simply could not do it, despite our genuine intention to care for ourselves in the best ways possible. These strategies are not neurotic or "unspiritual" or evidence that there is something wrong with us or that we're caught in a "low vibration"; they're just old ways of self-care that might be ripe for an update. The questions for each of us to explore are to what degree do we still require this type of protection, and how might these compensatory patterns be interfering with the type of life we are now wanting to live.

The reality for most of us is that we have capacities as adults that we did not have when our brains and nervous systems were developing, and we have access to more skillful, wise, and robust ways to care for ourselves that do not necessitate us keeping this old circuitry alive. It is a radical realization that we do not need to abandon ourselves to stay safe; in fact, the most unsafe thing we can do is to turn from ourselves when we need our own kindness and presence more than ever. It does take practice to train ourselves to tolerate and contain various levels of intensity and anxiety as we turn back toward that from which we've been conditioned to disconnect. But it is possible to discover—slowly and over time—new, creative, compassion-infused strategies to meet difficult experience when it comes.

To discover and implement a new way, we must first recognize when we are hooked and spinning into the old habitual modes of percep-tion. We cannot overwrite the conditioned pathways until there is awareness in the moment that we have become stuck. We can slow down and say to ourselves, "I can feel myself turning away, dropping into conditioned reactivity and familiar ways of turning from what is here now to be touched, held, and integrated. I am aware in this moment that without presence and self-compassion I will abandon myself in a moment of need. This time, just in this moment, I'm going to slow down, breathe deeply, ground into the earth, and choose a new way."

Often, especially in the beginning, when we "catch" ourselves falling down a hole, our immediate reaction will be one of subtle (or not-so-subtle) shame, blame, or self-aggression: "There I go again. Doing it wrong. Falling short, failing, getting hooked in that same pattern. What's wrong with me?" When we begin this work—or even if we are well practiced in it—at times it can appear we are becoming *more* neurotic and *more* of a mess and experiencing more triggered thoughts and feelings than ever. But this is usually not the case. Rather, we are finally slowing down and shining a spotlight—of curiosity, consciousness, and warmth—onto our experience, thereby illuminating that which has always been there.

These are important moments, when we catch ourselves before we fall down the rabbit hole and become flooded by our historical strategies to bail out of our immediate experience. Rather than beating ourselves up over this, we can see it is nothing short of a miracle that we have catalyzed enough awareness in the moment to see what is happening and to pause. This is a profound moment, and although the mind might tell us it's not really that big of a deal, in the heart and in the nervous system it is minor (or major) revolution. With many small moments of this sort of reorganization, we begin to replace that habitual shaming and blaming with curiosity. "Wow, everything was going just fine, and then all of a sudden I became completely caught in an avalanche of thought and feeling, spinning out and raging and shaming, attacking myself and blaming others. I'm going to slow down now and really listen, feel, sense, hold. I'm not going to abandon myself. Not in *this* moment, anyway." Over time, we learn to catch ourselves earlier and earlier in the process, before we have totally been swallowed up by the habitual reactivity of shame, blame, and self-aggression.

As we see and feel and sense this happening in the moment, with kindness we slowly turn back toward ourselves *in just this one moment* and choose something different.

In response to this invitation, many of us naturally say, "There is no way I can do this" as we sense into the future and wonder how we will ever change the patterns of a lifetime. But if we can begin in just *this* moment, and realize it is only in *this* moment we are asked to stay with, befriend, and bring compassion to, we leave the disembodied, unworkable future and discover the utter workability of this moment as it is. It doesn't mean we like it or are even "good" at it; neither of those are required, just the intention to care for yourself in a new way.

Slowly, over time, in small doses, we can begin to replace the old with the new, train ourselves to tolerate more and more, and truly start to befriend ourselves and our experience in ways previously not possible. Even though we might *feel* on the brink of overwhelm, nevertheless we are still here, still breathing, feet on the ground, hands on our heart, and senses online. Even though it might not *feel* safe, it *is* safe in the present moment to tend to yourself with love, compassion, kindness, and care. The feeling of unsafeness arises in the abandonment of ourselves; in turning from ourselves in moments when we need ourselves more than ever; in old strategies of freezing, dissociation, and disembodiment, once intelligent responses to the threat of total psychic overwhelm. Rather than engage the well-worn circuits to provide cover and relief, with practice and over time we return into that unknown middle place, where true healing is to be found.

UNTANGLING THE UNWORTHY ONE

One of the most important purposes of inner work is to illuminate the unconscious beliefs that shape the way we see ourselves, others, and the world. We carry these beliefs in a narrative (as well as in our cell tissue) that originated as our brain and nervous system were developing, in our attempt to make meaning of early relational experiences and how they affected our emerging sense of self.

If our early environment did not provide adequate holding as well as sufficient space for us to rest in unstructured states of being—if our unique subjectivity, emotional experience, and basic goodness were not effectively mirrored back to us—we found ourselves in a precarious place. As noted earlier, because it is just too unsafe to see this failed mirroring as resulting from a lack of capacity in those around us, we place the blame inside ourselves. We come to believe, in our attempt to make sense of our experience, that we're just not worthy of that sort of attention, affection, love, and attunement. As painful as this realization is, it provided a temporary refuge from overwhelming anxiety.

The chronic sense of shame so many of us experience in large part has its origins in backgrounds lacking in empathic attunement, where there was no adequate holding environment in which our little nervous systems could unfold, rest, and explore in a way that would foster true self-love. The narrative of the unworthy one is deeply embedded and spans multiple levels: cognitive, emotional, neurobiological, somatic, and behavioral. In addition to these conventional levels of experience, there are also vast implications at the spiritual, or transpersonal, level because these early organizations of experience seem to provide a temporary filter over the discovery of what many contemplative traditions refer to as our true nature, the part of us that is always already whole and was never unhealed. We must send breath, awareness, and love into each of these areas to transform the compensatory identity structure and to untangle the wounds of the body and the heart.

Although it might seem impossible because it is so deeply embedded, this narrative can be reauthored. It can be rewritten. It can be updated. A more cohesive, real-time, accurate, integrated story can be told. A new dream can be dreamed. New cloth can be woven. It is possible. I have been honored to witness this reorganization in the lives of many courageous women and men over the years. It is not easy work and asks everything of us. It is so important to remind each other of this revolutionary possibility, especially during times of profound suffering, and that there is hope. Although the narrative of shame and unworthiness can feel so entrenched—and the corresponding feelings so overwhelming—it is possible to replace the pathways of abandonment and aggression with empathy and kindness. Over time the traumatic narrative can be recrafted, new meaning can be discovered, and new life can be found. New breath can be breathed. Even in the core of the most profound hopelessness, a small light of hope is buried there, and the flame is still alive.

This is not some Pollyannaish or overly romantic, positivistic fantasy. Of course, none of us know, certainly including myself, if *everyone* can heal, transform, and find a way out of profound trauma and pain. Although some people claim that all suffering serves an intelligent purpose and exists for our ultimate spiritual benefit, I think it's important to explore these ideas with as much nuance and depth as we can. For some, yes, suffering can provide a powerful vehicle through which healing and transformation can occur. But others are not so fortunate, and their pain creates devastation in the personality from which they do not always recover. Understanding the mysteries of one's karma, destiny, and purpose is most certainly beyond my pay grade. At some point, all we can really do is share our own experience, which, for me, is of the outrageous intelligence and bravery of the broken human heart and its ability to return home, to discover the light that can so easily become buried within the dark.

THE TERRITORY OF GRIEF

The process of grieving is highly individual and can never be pinned down in some clinical or philosophical formula. To provide sanctuary and safe passage for the wound, we must discover our own way to navigate and tend to difficulty, loss, and pain. But how this looks and especially the time frame in which it unfolds is a matter of one's own unique path. Although some kindred travelers have provided maps and signposts into the unlit places and darkened corridors of the psyche, they are not always nuanced or specific enough for our individual journeys. Let us take in the wisdom of the mapmakers with an open mind and grateful heart, while at the same time remembering that the maps are *not* the territory, especially in the realms of soul. We need not conform our journey to another's, and, in fact, by trying to do so, we dishonor the radical uniqueness of the path for us, which is ours alone to walk and might not always look like that of another.

The appearance of grief—including its cognitive, emotional, somatic, and behavioral manifestations—might erupt at a moment of loss, or we could cycle back to it over and over again throughout our lives, for example, each time we hear a certain piece of music, see a particular color in a sunset, or sense a certain feeling or fragrance. We reenter into that movement of the heart known as grief. At times, we are quite aware of "what" we are grieving, whereas at other times the grief is more general and free-floating, and we find ourselves breaking open for reasons we cannot quite pin down. Although it is tempting to attribute feelings of anguish to a specific situation in our lives, it is not always possible to do this because at times we are asked to hold a different sort of grief, perhaps for another person, for an animal friend, for the earth, or for the soul of the world.

In my experience, grief is not something we "get over" by following prescribed stages but something we might be asked to tend to throughout our lives. It is individual and takes a unique expression for each person. The psychiatric community, insurance companies, and well-intentioned teachers and healers cannot predict the timeline for this voyage; it is written in the stars. To pathologize the experience of grief is to work against nature.

The grieving process might not have an endpoint, a goal line, or state of completion in which we come to some final resolution, "finish," and land in some untouchable place, free from falling apart yet again. Although some forms of spirituality and healing have this fantasied end state as a targeted objective, the heart is endless and grief might become a companion for the duration of a life, a kindred traveler into the depths, revealing light the nongrieving state could never contain. For me, it is not so much a process as a nonlinear, unfolding partner. It moves not by way of a straight line but by that of circle and spiral.

This image of the spiral and sense of an unfolding process circling the material of our lives is a rich imaginative lens through which to vision the unique journey we are on. At times, it can be incredibly frustrating and repetitive because we spin around the same themes without it seeming like there is much movement. At other times, we encounter some crack where the light breaks in; what seemed at first glance a mere repetition is somehow different, revealing a piece of the mystery we couldn't quite see at an earlier time. The alchemists called this spiral the *circulatio*, or *rotatio*, a sacred process involving touching and retouching the heart, the material of our lives. We circle or rotate around the essential themes unique to us that form the *prima materia* of our own personal opus. From an alchemical perspective, although we might not appear to be making any progress and might seem stuck, appearances can be deceiving.

Even if we no longer grieve the sense of a personal loss, we might be asked by forces larger than ourselves to grieve for the ancestors, the ones yet to come, and the earth and her creatures. At some point, perhaps we can no longer discern between our own grief and that of a galaxy being born and dying. Grieving is not only personal but cultural, historical, and archetypal. As it humbles and purifies, it opens a portal into the mystery.

LETTING GO OF LETTING GO

In some contemporary teachings, we are frequently asked to "let go" of difficult states of mind that we do not like, with the underlying assumption that they stand in the way of healing and self-realization, as obstacles on the path. "Letting go" has become the battle cry of much personal development work, especially as applied to psychic material deemed invalid by a more transcendent orientation to "growth" and upward movement (we usually associate "growing" with up, not down into the shadow, body, and depths). Up and out the material goes, to some other dimension, place, realm, or abode where we're safe from feeling, from further vulnerability, and from our hearts breaking, to a place of "mastery" and power and manifesting all the things we (think we) want and need to make us happy. It's understandable, really. It's an alluring promise.

Practitioners of this orientation, in ways that can be subtle and hidden under the surface, argue that anger is bad, confusion is a sign we've failed, fear is the "opposite" of love, and so forth. Even some ancient wisdom teachings tell us that anger is a stain on who we are and that we need to eliminate it; it is in and of itself the cause of our suffering and struggle. But anger is not the problem; *what we do with the anger* is the (potential) problem. If we have a theoretical view that anger "is" bad, how are we likely to respond when it inevitably comes up in our lives, in our own experience, and in those around us? We all know the tragic consequences of a culture that represses anger; that has pathologized rage; that is unable to tolerate, contain, and skillfully tend to the ordinary waves of human aggression—not to mention has forgotten how to mine anger's healthy expression, for example, in setting effective boundaries, protecting our own integrity, and standing up for ourselves (and others) in the face of psychological, emotional, or physical abuse and neglect. We need only look around at the tragedy of mass school shootings or other senseless violence to see how our world is calling out for an embodied, mature, and authentic relationship to the natural experience of anger.

Certain feelings and states are conceived as being of a "low vibration" that keeps us trapped in some darkened dimension of experience, cut off from the great ascension that awaits all beings. "Just snap out of it, get out of that low vibration, it's just your 'ego.'" The idea behind the scenes seems to be that after we are enlightened, fear will be replaced by love, jealousy by openness, and heartbreak by joy. The grand spiritual replacement project marches on. But where is all this leading?

As a result of this aggressive campaign against various unwanted bands of the emotional spectrum, an array of valid (and intelligent) energies, messengers, and figures get pushed further into the shadow *where they will eventually leak out*, usually in ways that extend suffering for ourselves and others. This leaking happens at personal, cultural, and collective levels, and if we continue to deny, repress, or stuff our emotional experience, it will only gain power in the unconscious.

The alchemists were always on the lookout for and warning against a "leaky vessel," meaning that critical aspects of the material seeped out of the container in which they were working. Rather than prematurely "letting go" of this material—an understandable position given the difficulty in staying with, working through, and metabolizing it—an alternative invitation is to cultivate a conscious relationship with it so that we do not inadvertently project it onto others and into the world in a way that generates more struggle, confusion, violence, and pain. For as the relational analysts have discovered, that which we are not able to access, articulate, contain, and work through, we will inevitably evoke in others, enact within the interactional field, locate outside of ourselves, or discover within our own bodies.

As with all medicines and approaches, there is wisdom in letting go (just as there is wisdom in "staying in the present moment," "forgiving those who have harmed us," and "accepting reality the way it is"); however, we must go slowly and not oversimplify things, which leads to a generalized, abstract relationship with these teachings that is secondhand and not sensitive enough to our lived, unique experience.

STEPPING OFF THE BATTLEFIELD

As with all spiritual beliefs and practices, the act of "letting go" can serve wisdom, and it can also serve distraction and avoidance. Through experimentation and intuition, we must make these subtle discernments in the fire of our own direct experience. It is important to explore our motivation to engage certain forms of inner work, including the intention to "let go" of some aspect of our inner experience. What it would mean to slow down and to "let go" of an intense emotion, a painful memory, an old trauma, or a current self-image? Where would it go? What would we gain? What would replace it? What would all this accomplish? What are we actually talking about?

To be clear, I'm not suggesting that we jettison the concept of "letting go" but bring it into the fire of our inquiry, where we can allow its subtle qualities and essences to clarify. In my clinical work I have seen how the project of "letting go" can be yet another manifestation of unconscious self-aggression and abandonment of parts of ourselves not acceptable in our families of origin or to our developing personas. In this sense, the demand that we "let certain experiences go" is merely a painful reenactment of the way important figures reacted to our emotional world at an earlier time in our developmental history: "Just get over it. Snap out of it. Stop crying. We've given you everything, so stop being so sad. Don't you dare get angry with me. Stop being such a baby. When will you be like [fill in best friend's name here]? S/he would never do that. How could you let me down again? Stop being so scared! Be grateful for what you have and stop complaining!" Any of that sound familiar?

Of course, in the contemporary self-help world, the language is usually much more spiritual, but often the underlying prescription is the same—dissolve your fear, replace it with love; forgive everyone and let that wash away your anger; don't be heartbroken because we're all one anyway; get out of your ego and into your higher self; get out of that "low vibration" and lame third-dimensional orientation—ascend now into the fourth, fifth, or sixth, and so forth. Again, it's not to say there is no truth underlying these concepts; however, it is the shadow side which is often left out. We must illuminate and integrate the shadow into our inquiry if what we want is a full-spectrum, embodied, fully human relationship with these ideas and realizations.

By approaching psychic experience and aspects of our emotional, mental, physical, and spiritual bodies through the lens of "letting go," we can subtly and unconsciously reinforce the neural pathways of previous empathic failure and the circuitry of shame, in which we end up attacking our own vulnerability in ways remarkably similar to the way it was met when we were younger. This is not to say that all forms and approaches to "letting go" are oriented in this psychic patterning but only an invitation, as always, into deeper levels of discernment. It's an invitation to clarify our intention for wanting or needing to "let something go," what that would actually mean in our experience, and how we think it would benefit us to do so. Before we engage in any practice, including that of "letting go," let us do so from a grounded and illuminated place.

Rather than "letting go" of difficult emotions, at times we are invited to step off the battlefield and turn back toward them, curious about why these visitors have come, what messages they might have for us, as we begin to relate to our internal world as a retinue of allies come to guide us into the depths. We are never going to unearth the intimacy, connection, and freedom for which we yearn as long as we are subtly at war with parts of ourselves, deeming them invalid and acting to purge them from the larger field of awareness that we are. We must discover for ourselves whether their mere presence or our abandonment and rejection of them is the root cause of our suffering and struggle.

Let us rest together as we come to the end of this chapter and allow a few moments to integrate the journey we've been on. As we turn toward that alive middle territory in-between the extremes and provide sanctuary and safe passage for our grief, shame, and the entire land-scape of feeling to return to its home in the heart, we begin to care for ourselves in a new way, rooted in curiosity, compassion, and a fiery love of the truth. As our inquiry deepens, our confidence continues to build, and that no matter what is happening in our lives, we can trust in our capacity to meet what is there with newfound levels of presence and kindness and respond in more and more skillful ways.

4

A SACRED DEFLATION

Working with the Inevitable Experiences of Uncertainty, Disappointment, and Loss

IN THIS CHAPTER, WE'LL EXPLORE THE common themes of disappointment and loss, which on the surface can appear formidable obstacles in our path, seeming to obscure the peace and joy we yearn for, serving as daunting impediments to our deepest longing. As always, however, we must go into the depths and seek illumination and renewed vision, for in the core of these experiences is intelligence and guidance, even unexpected grace, that can be mined only in their center. We don't usually associate the word "deflation" with something positive in our lives; however, as we deepen our capacity to befriend ourselves and our experience and infuse it with more penetrating levels of curiosity, awareness, and compassion, we might come to experience deflation as an ally as we unearth its unexpected wisdom.

It's natural to have a bias for the experience of "success" over "failure," whatever those ideas have come to mean for us. But let us be conscious of this predisposition and not fall into fragmentation. Whether in the outer world of accomplishments or in the inner world of collecting experiences, learning to fail *consciously* opens us to the full spectrum. There are secret jewels in failure not accessible by way of success, but we must cleanse our perception to mine the gold hidden there. Inside the contraries of success and failure is a doorway, a parting of the veil, revealing an unknown reality of newfound creativity. Although it is tempting to remain on one side of the door—or the other—the invitation, as we've been exploring together, is into the alive, yet not fully known middle territory, which will require an inevitable confrontation and integration of the opposing energies so that a new, third way can reveal itself.

We live in a world that has lost contact with the evolutionary potential of conscious dissolution, deflation, and the inevitable disappointment we each face as we journey along the way. These experiences are not mistakes or errors to be corrected, cured, or fixed, for they are too holy for that. The art of allowing things to fall apart and honoring the death aspect of the death-rebirth journey is one known by alchemists, mystics, and poets but is not popular in a culture obsessed with persona and happiness at all costs and with the fantasy of invulnerability, untouchability, and consistent feelings of joy and peace.

The alchemists referred to this stage of the psyche as the *nigredo*, or blackened state. Despite the possibility of future stages of light, transmutation, white, yellow, and red (leading up to the discovery of the mysterious philosopher's stone), the *nigredo* is pure on its own. It has its own interiority, depth, and meaning, bearing messages, gifts, and visions not available in lighter and brighter stages. Its value is found in its own subjective core, not merely in its function as the preparatory phase for greater (whiter) things to come. In religious language, the *nigredo* is the dark night of the soul, the creative potential of the blackness and separation, which is painful and purifying as it removes or putrefies (*putrefactio*) what has come to make way for the new to emerge. It would be uncommon in our conventional world to view the process of putrefaction as holy, even sacred, but it comes as an expression of the divine, or the beloved, as darkened midwife to the deep interior.

This cyclical activity is the essence of creativity and is nonnegotiable in human experience as well as in the natural world, a symbol and archetypal image of the energy (love) that keeps the stars from falling out of the sky. This process reveals that the old must be recycled, decomposed, and turned into fertilizer to produce the soil required for the new to take birth. The qualities of this soil are the same qualities that form the cells of the human heart, the nature of which we must discover in our own unique ways. We can try to fight against this organic movement, which we often do, abandoning the energies of reorganization in hopes of keeping the old forms alive. But as many have discovered—in a way both heartbreaking and purifyingly humbling—this battle will be lost. It's a holy loss, though, as the consequences of denying the creative activity of dissolution are a life of partiality and flatness and a heart that longs (endlessly) for life.

If we will not consciously carry the energies of failure, deflation, and disappointment, they remain in seed form in the shadow and *will* erupt, usually in unskillful ways that lead to chaotic experiences for ourselves and others. This is true not only for individuals but also for couples, families, groups, cultures, societies, and countries. The wide-ranging consequences of how this material is tended is why many consider shadow work not only necessary for one's own psychological and spiritual growth but also an ethical responsibility to the world and life everywhere. (I'll speak more about the shadow in chapter 8.)

Through our willingness to contain, hold, and care for the entirety of what we are, we will know the reality of the sacred world. The invitation, as always, is not to something partial but to *full* participation in success, to *full* participation in failure, and to knowing the ineffable third dimension we experience in the core of the unresolvable dance between these seemingly contradictory poles of experience. Out of this experiential knowing we naturally surround the figures and energies of our unlived lives with our presence, hold them and provide sanctuary for their conscious integration, dissolving the trance of partiality and revealing essence.

It is not easy to navigate and play in these relational fields until our perception is cleansed because the dream is thick and deeply embedded. Fortunately, as I will continue to repeat, this work requires only *one* moment, *this* one, and cannot be completed in the past or future. Only now. No matter what is happening in the inner and outer landscape, we can all begin right now. And now. And now. And even now.

CREATIVE DISSOLUTION

In each moment the sacred process of death and rebirth is playing out within us. With each breath, something in us is dying—some aspect of who we think we are or what we're doing here, a relationship we were sure would last forever, the work or spiritual path that once brought us meaning, consistent health in our physical bodies, an idea about how it was all going to turn out.

In the face of this dissolution, the question isn't so much how we can most quickly facilitate rebirth *but to what degree we will participate in the death when it appears*. Psychological death, or spiritual death, is not just a preliminary process in which we engage so that we can put it behind us and get on to birth. It is a valid, honorable, holy unfolding in its own right, with its own interiority, dimensionality, and intelligence, as the alchemists remind us through their conceptualization and experience of the *nigredo*. It is not just a way station from which the new is launched but a container, catalyst, and vessel of insight, perspective, and revelation that can never be found within the state of birth. It is perfectly natural to trust that rebirth will occur, but let us do so while staying embodied during the death aspect of the journey, the dissolving of form, which carries its own sacredness and integrity.

In times of transition, our tendency is to rush to rebirth, quickly back into the known, in an urgent attempt to cure, maintain, or heal that which is dying, that which longs to transform. However, death does not need to be cured or healed but lived and touched and experienced fully. It is natural to resist falling apart and do what we can to put it all back together. It's so human, really. But it is only from the womb of death—attuned to consciously—that rebirth can emerge. Inside death are the raw materials for new life, and any birth that occurs without tending to the creativity buried within the dissolution will be partial.

The invitation, which at times we can hear clearly—during the dark of night, in the slowness and the depths, in silence in nature, as we move in and out of states of sleep and dream—is not to abandon death in our rush to be reborn, not to short-circuit the intelligence and creativity that is death, and to remember that rebirth is not possible without the creativity of dissolution.

Allow the death some time to unfold, to share its poetry and fragrance, not partial but whole. Death is not merely a phase to get through as quickly as possible en route to new life but is pure and complete on its own, with wisdom and perspective not available during times of birth. In those periods in our lives, when things are being rearranged and reorganized inside and around us, we can attune to what is truly being asked, whether it is to cure death and reassemble the known or to allow the forms of love safe passage to continue their journey. We can listen to the wisdom in death and what it has to teach us about love and helping others and this world.

During times of transition, grief, and loss, we are asked to honor the forms of love as they come into our lives and touch us and share their beauty. But equally we allow them to dissolve so that new forms can emerge and provide the healing and transformation for which we most deeply long.

We can give these forms permission to dance and play and also to move on and continue their journey without us. We can grieve with or without them, with the stars and oceans and moons as our witnesses.

THE PURITY OF REORGANIZATION

A certain death occurs as part of the healing process; in the deepening of self-awareness, something does not survive illumination. There is a fantasy that we can come out the other side intact, without having to sacrifice some aspect of ourselves in the fires of transformation. But it doesn't really seem to work this way, not with lasting and deep healing. Although it is tempting to spin out of the uncertainty and into rebirth as quickly as possible, as I've suggested, there is wisdom and purity within the reorganization itself that we cannot know if we abandon it prematurely.

When we engage in any work of depth, we inevitably come up against a cultural bias toward the light, the upward, and the bright-ened dimensions of the path. Although the journey invites us to touch, travel, and explore across the entire spectrum, we cannot sidestep or bypass the darkened condition, those parts of psyche buried and hidden beneath ordinary awareness. We're not going to *want* to go into these areas of the personality—our core vulnerabilities, shadow parts, painful feelings, inconsistencies, selfishness, unmet narcissism, and tendencies toward self-absorption. Especially if we identify as a spiritual person cultivating the light, kind, compassionate, giving, selfless, grateful, for-giving, at peace, and not ever caught in the so-called negative emotions of fear, rage, jealousy, and depression, this turning into the dark can be quite challenging. In any event, we can't wait around until we *feel* like doing it, until we're open to it, until we can accept it all, or until we feel inspired. Somehow, we must find the curiosity, courage, and energy to engage this dimension of experience *even if we don't want to.*

Seen with eyes wide open, the dissolution (which can occur by way of the alchemical *solutio* or *putrefactio*) is initiation because it offers vision not available from within the clear, reflected, held-together state. It is as if an ancient part of ourselves, a kindred traveler who has accompanied us for so long, is no longer permitted to continue the journey by our side. The old dream crumbles—"my life" and the way I was sure it was going to turn out. This prior soul companion might be another person or an inner traveler—a feeling, memory, idea, or image through which we'd been seeing ourselves and others; any emotionally significant part of our world that has finished its time here.

To go through the initiation and fully participate in the creativity of the death-rebirth cycle, we must slow down; return into the earth; and listen to the music, poetry, and high-voltage guidance found in the depths. Yes, there might always be an urgency to overcome the dissolution and get to the next phase as quickly as possible. But wisdom in the dark is preparing the vessel for the next illumination. The invitation is to allow the old to wash away and to grieve the way you thought it was all going to turn out. This grief is holy and opens the heart to imagination and revisioning.

As tempting as it might be, we cannot skip stages. Take some time to mourn the reassembling of your world and provide safe passage for all that you will inevitably lose as you heal and awaken. In times of transition, what is here now is often unclear, uncertain, and unknown. From the conventional perspective, these psychic states are not usually envisioned as rich, meaningful, and valid in their own right but merely as "processes" to get through, ideally as quickly as possible, so that we can return to life and the next series of accumulations and births. Or they are fantasized to be of a "lower vibration," which only places them deeper into the personal and collective shadow.

Upon closer examination, these states are awash with meaning and wisdom, but to stay with them and unearth those qualities, our perception must be reorganized. New images, new myths, new lenses must emerge through which we can navigate a new world. Even more than those, a shift of the heart is most required, a willingness to befriend ourselves at levels previously not thought possible. If we are interested in feeling alive, in tapping into the creativity within us, and in fully participating in the sacred world, we must revision the model that pathologizes the darkness and the moon and glorifies the sun and the light. Inside the body is a temple that reveals the union of opposites; a sanctuary where they dance and play, fall apart, and hold it all together; a secret place where they meet as one.

THE WISDOM AT THE CORE

Again, let us look to the alchemical *prima materia* to guide us here. The alchemists were in search of this sacred substance, which had to be located before the work could start. Until the primary material was identified and isolated, the alchemical opus could not begin. It is like that in our own lives. We must clarify what in any given moment is most wanting and needing our attention, awareness, care, and love. We start there *even if we do not want to*, even if it feels icky and meaningless and unspiritual. The intelligence in the heart brings forward the *prima materia* for us if we slow down and open into the unknown. Remember, we might never *want* to go into this material, for it has come to be associated with the unworkable, overwhelming, and potentially devastating, unworthy, irredeemable—evidence of our neurosis, selfishness, narcissism, or failure. Somehow, we must overcome this momentum and see for ourselves if tending to this *prima materia* is *actually* unsafe in our here-and-now adult experience as it likely was in our developmental history. We must go slowly, at times *very* slowly—one microsecond at a time—and honor the realities of our hearts and nervous systems. But at the same time we push ourselves just a little and see.

As always, it can help to explore difficult thoughts, feelings, memories, images, and bodily sensations alongside an attuned other who can help us to create a strong-enough, safe-enough, and sacred-enough container to hold the material without the vessel or our nervous systems breaking. Of course, it is not always possible to do this with another, and there are times when we will be asked to walk alone. Even if you do not have another to enter into the vessel with you, know that you are never *truly* alone. There are beings everywhere who are doing this work and opening their hearts in this same way, who alternate between feelings of fear and encouragement, excitement and terror, clarity and confusion, hopelessness and hope. These ones are with you and you with them in the relational field and you can feel them, love them, be loved by them, hold them, and be held by them in nonphysical ways.

In archetypal psychology, we are invited to see through the appearance of our emotional affliction and into its mythological core, to the gods or goddesses responsible for a particular complex, symptom, or realm of psychic experience.[1] To do so can help us see beyond the personal weight of the difficult thoughts and feelings and allow them to be held in a larger context, opening ourselves to a deeper layer of meaning and purpose. In a similar way, in the Vajrayana Buddhist tradition, the five primordial Buddhas each watch over emotions with which they are associated.[2] Whether I'm referring to Greek gods or Tibetan deities, my invitation here is not to believe in any of this in a literal way (please feel free to do so or not) but to step into an imaginal realm where wisdom energies dwell inside the core of even our most difficult experience. The invitation is to allow in the possibility that there is tremendous intelligence and creativity within our symptoms that we can mine and release by infusing the material with awareness, curiosity, and compassion.

There is information in our symptoms, a certain intelligence or creativity evidenced in the way psyche manifests in our thoughts, feelings, bodily sensations, images, fantasies, and dreams. By turning toward the symptom and tending to it with presence, warmth, and kindness, we are able to unearth the unique wisdom found only there. No matter how the *prima materia* appears for us—as a difficult relationship, challenging health diagnosis, unexpected depression, profound boredom, or loss and transition—we can begin to "heat" the material and create the conditions under which its hidden meaning and intelligence may emerge. Although this "heat" is unique for each of us, it is none other than love itself. But what this "love" looks and feels and moves like in our experience is something we must discover for ourselves. A second-hand fire will never do.

The alchemists viewed the *prima materia* as sacred, holy, and the substance of the gods, given uniquely to each of us at a specific time to further the great work of unfolding consciousness. Even though this material can be quite challenging, it is not merely something to let go of, transcend, or replace. When we're able to enter into its core, what we discover is neither neurosis nor pathology. It is not something to cure, fix, or even "heal" but a portal deep into the vessel of our own psyches. The invitation roaring within this passageway is into friendship, intimacy, and cleansed perception. It is not always going to *feel* safe or comfortable to do this because we are hardwired to turn from the pain and the uncertainty and return to safe ground. We can honor this call back to homeostasis at times—as a valid and appropriate choice in a given moment of our experience or time in our lives—whereas at other times, we can take the risk of moving closer to ourselves with curiosity, interest, and love. This work is an ongoing journey, cultivated in each here-and-now moment, not a destination at which we one day arrive and are done. Neither is it an urgent race to the finish line. There is no urgency on the path of the heart.

If in a given moment, we are met with fear, worry, anger, or shame, the invitation is to first slow down, recognize that a visitor has come, and renew the ancient vow we once made that for *just this one moment,* we will not abandon ourselves. As we all know, it can take quite a lot of focus, energy, and presence not to fall down into the quicksand of overwhelm and claustrophobia, where we become flooded and swallowed up by the feelings and associated thoughts, memories, and impulses. It can be challenging to cut that momentum of habitual consciousness, whether it comes by way of repression, dissociation, or being aggressive toward ourselves and realize, "Oh, I'm hooked. I'm triggered. There it is. Another opportunity has been given."

Just this one simple instant of recognition can cut into billions of moments of turning away. We can begin to reframe these emotionally saturated moments not as ones of failure, in which we've been neurotically activated yet again, but as ones of gratitude and opportunity: somehow *this time* we've been able to see; to stay close; not to get caught completely; and to bring in awareness, space, and perspective. We can recognize the miracle of pausing, slowing down, and at least contemplating the possibility of choosing a different path. In so doing, we reorganize our perception, revisioning and reframing what is happening so as to see that in this moment the *prima materia* is presenting itself. It is arising here and now, in this moment, *not* to obscure or obstruct our path as an enemy to take us down but as some sort of ally, albeit a fierce and uninvited one. This is a sacred moment. It doesn't mean we like it or love it or want it to continue or even that we force ourselves to "accept" it. It is sacred because it serves a holy function, one of revelation. And it is an ally because we have met the visitor in a new way, with some curiosity, mindfulness, openness, and warmth, and in an unexpected way it is helping us to lay down a new groove in our tender nervous system and raw, open heart.

It's not easy to do this when our emotional world is on fire—to slow down and recognize that we've been hooked, to reframe what is happening and see that what is here now is valid, that it is the way psyche is expressing itself in this moment and can be respected. It is purposive, even if we are unable to know or articulate its precise purpose or function in the moment. It is a radical new way of trusting in ourselves and even our most disturbing experience. With practice, slowly, over time, we *can* catch ourselves in these moments with increasing awareness and self-compassion before the avalanche of feeling takes us down. Even if we only notice it one second earlier than we normally would, that is a miracle, really. Then two seconds. Then three. At some point we might start to realize that we notice and articulate the activation *as it arises*—just as the anger, shame, rage, despair, criticism, and self-aggression appear, we are there to meet and receive it. It appears within a larger context of awareness and is apprehended and held as an utterly workable, valid part of our self, as a mine of wisdom filled with important information for the way ahead. This doesn't mean it's not painful or we won't fall back down or slip up or forget or have to start over. But, slowly, we continue building this new skill and neural groove of slowness, empathy, and spaciousness. And over time, it begins to become second nature, not requiring so much practice and effort. But that happens at a pace and according to a timeline unique for each of us.

THE COURAGE TO PARTICIPATE

As part of our work with the *prima materia* of our lives, we must be increasingly aware of conditioning that tells us that the mere appearance of difficult emotions is evidence some problem has occurred; there is some error or mistake we must urgently move to correct; we "should" be feeling joy, happiness, gratitude, and bliss; the emotional activation is the result of our being stuck in a "low vibration"; or we have lost contact with some magical law or secret of the universe and should quickly start to think different thoughts. Embracing and befriending the *prima materia* is the end of self-abandonment and self-aggression, when we are no longer willing to turn from ourselves and our vulnerability in those times when we need ourselves more than ever. Pain is not pathology.[3] Emotion is not pathology. They are revealers and allies of the path, but we must slow down and reorient with fresh vision, as beginners curious about what it is like to fully participate in our experience, stay with ourselves, and open to the wisdom within us.

In a larger sense, this is *courage*, that willingness to discover what the *prima materia* is for *you* (which can of course change over time, and even within the same day) and to honor, care about, and dare I say even *love* it. This is not some manufactured love or a certain feeling state of sweetness and peace. It is fierce and alive and has nothing to do with whether we even *like* what we discover. The alchemists loved the material they worked with and recognized that it was filled with soul, with its own subjectivity, perspective, and beingness. For them, entering into the vessel with the material was a love affair to which they gave everything. This love of the psyche, taking a risk to trust (over time) what it produces, is such an important part of the journey. We must each discover what this "love" looks like for us, beyond a mere concept, in our actual, lived, embodied experience. What would it possibly mean to "love" our heartbreak, our sadness, our confusion, our feeling down? What would it mean to open our hearts to our experience in a new way? Even if we do not "like" what we are experiencing and wish it were different, there is a deeper invitation into an unconditional love we might discover as we deepen our work. We love *reality*, and this is how it appears in this moment.

No matter what is happening in our lives—the ups and downs and pain and joy and struggle and beauty and grief—this is the *prima materia*. We can start exactly where we are; in fact, that is the *only* place we can start. In this sense, courage is not so much a feeling state that comes and goes but a passion and interest in what is here, in what has been given, in the intelligence of psyche. It is a longing to know yourself, to know the material of your life, even to be friends with those parts of yourself on which you had given up or otherwise turned away from and shamed.

It really is a conundrum, this being human: we want to heal, but we don't want to be too vulnerable, take too much risk, or turn toward the shaky, raw, unguarded life sure to be there to greet us when we open into a new way of being. Yes, we might feel some excitement about the whole thing—imagination of a life beyond conditioning—but how do we weigh that against our intuitive knowing of what will be required to transform perception and wake up out of old and outmoded ways of being?

We do not find the freedom we long for in our attempts to resolve this conundrum but in attuning to the creativity at its core. Our felt sense of freedom arises naturally when we begin to perceive the contradictions of the psyche as carriers of sacred life energy, revealing a mystery beyond the conscious mind's capacity to understand. The true nature of freedom makes itself apparent when we dare to see that the beloved, or love—or God or nature or Life or Source—is not separate from this conundrum but is taking form *as the conundrum itself*. In fact, it *is* His or Her actual body. It is not some cosmic error or mistake we must remedy by means of process or improvement but a pure emanation of wisdom itself. The contradictions have been placed inside us as a gift and benediction, the *prima materia* for us to work with, the exact material that has come into the vessel for tending and heating with our passion, interest, and commitment. The faithfulness and allegiance is not primarily to shifting, changing, transforming, or even healing but to *participating*, to infusing the material with our presence, to wanting more than anything to get to know it, take it as a lover, and dance with it as a way to embrace the mystery.

COMING FROM A PLACE OF TRUE COMPASSION

As an example of this *prima materia* and approaching ("heating") it in a curious, inquiring, and compassionate way, let us explore a common emotional experience many of us have and struggle with—that of disappointing another person, especially someone who means a lot to us or whom we look up to, depend upon, or with whom we are in conflict. Discomfort and anxiety about disappointing another can loom large in our relationships and can present itself as some challenging material with which to engage. In fact, many have come to organize much of their experience around this particular dynamic, doing whatever it takes *never* to allow this to happen, doing whatever they must to ensure they never let anyone down—and if it does happen, moving urgently to recover the status quo. If we are drawn, we can experiment with bringing curiosity and awareness to the feelings, beliefs, and vulnerabilities that constellate when we (inevitably) trigger disappointment in another, when we are unable to live up to their expectations, when we cannot see or hold them as they long to be seen and held, or when we fail to help or be there for them in the way they are asking. When we slowly start to invite these images, beliefs, feelings, and sensations into conscious awareness, we can meet them with deeper levels of seeing and compassion.

At times we face the decision, often in the moment, whether to set a boundary with another—when they are struggling, enraged, on the attack, or deeply depressed—or whether to meet them in the thick of it and help them to regulate the fire moving through them. This can be a difficult choice and requires a lot of experimentation as well as willingness to do it in a way not perceived as "right." The invitation is to be as authentic, transparent, and kind as we can, recognizing that the most skillful and compassionate response might be *not* to engage but to take space, say no, assert our own needs, and act (even forcefully) in the moment to protect our own integrity. The reality is that at times we choose (as an adult, not as a child becoming a doormat in the avoidance of difficult feelings) to move toward others, to engage directly with them, and to help them soothe the difficulty they are experiencing. At other times the most authentic, skillful, and compassionate response is to say, "I love you. I hate that you're suffering. *And* I cannot be there for you right now in the way you need." No apology, no shaming ourselves, no self-attack, no self-judgment. Just a clear, adult decision in the moment. And then the willingness to feel whatever feelings come and not see them as evidence that we have failed or made the "wrong" decision.

Of course, part of us wants to be there 100 percent of the time, removing the pain, "being compassionate," not avoiding intimacy, not shutting down, being a good partner, not being lost in our own self-absorption, being a kind person, being capable of handling all situations, and so forth. But the unconscious motivation behind this must be explored. Is our intention to be there for another coming from true compassion, or is it merely the reenactment of a little one scrambling for any possible tie to a fleeing or dysregulated attachment figure in an earlier time? Am I truly caring for the situation—for myself and the other—or simply replaying a historical pattern in which my only choice was to deny my own integrity and privilege the needs of another?

As is often the case with complex emotional situations, the answer to these questions is not black or white but a more nuanced (alchemical) grey in which part of our motivation is oriented in true compassion, in healthy and genuine care for the other, and in our skillful capacity in the moment to help them. Simultaneously, there might also be some remnants of the past alive and on the scene when we scramble to help as a way of regulating our own anxiety, pain of unworthiness, and fractured sense of self. In these situations, we are invited to honor the behaviors that come from healthy compassion and continue to cultivate and express them in ever more wise and skillful ways. We can challenge those less-than-healthy expressions, bring them out into the open with the light of kindness and awareness, and begin to tend to the underlying vulnerability needing extra attention. Rather than locating this material unconsciously in the other or the relational field itself, as an act of love we withdraw these projections, reown what is ours, and begin to infuse and heat it up with our own curiosity, care, and attunement.

A TEMPLATE OF EARLY CARETAKING

I'd like to end this chapter on deflation, loss, and disappointment by discussing a common early environmental situation that often goes unacknowledged because it is relevant for a lot of us and is related to these themes in a way that might not be obvious upon first glance. Many are put in the position of emotionally taking care of an adult early in their lives, at a time when they themselves need more than anything to have their own inner experience mirrored back to them. Even if our early environment was not solely organized around this dynamic, aspects of this patterning are alive in many of us. As part of our inquiry, we might discover remnants of this constellation and how it is affecting the way we perceive and relate to ourselves and others. For those influenced by this organization, a template is formed that, until compassionately illuminated with clear seeing, orients our sense of self and how we navigate close, personal relationships.

In these early configurations, the child's sense of self becomes tangled up in the other's moods, anxiety, dissatisfaction, and sense of well-being. The job of the little one is shifted from unstructured play and discovery into attending to the unlived life of a caretaker, a task not designed for a young nervous system or for a tender little heart coming to know itself and the world. It is confusing to children, however, because they have no real choice in the matter. They are wired to do whatever it takes to generate even a modicum of affection, attunement, and love. If the way they come to know this connection and positive sense of self-worth is through tending to the emotional world of the other, it sets up a painful, contradictory, and unworkable dilemma. Not knowing of any other possibility, they assume this is just the way things are and have no recourse other than to comply. All the while, their little soul is crushed under the weight of a task they were never designed to assume.

If we look carefully, we might see how this template lives and plays out in our lives as adults: in our fears around having or expressing needs; in fixation on whether we've disappointed someone and what it means about us as a person if we did; in the shakiness around allowing another to matter; in losing ourselves in fusion and codependence; and in being unable to assert our own needs, enact healthy boundaries, say no, or engage in appropriate conflict. We are caught in the terror of relationship, on the one hand, and in the painful longing for it, on the other; in the existential confusion around where we end and where the other begins; in the ancient conclusion that caring for another requires a deeply rooted disavowal of our own psyche, body, and heart.

To the degree this dynamic is alive within us, we come to see our own value through the changing emotional states of another, on guard at all times: "Have I disappointed them? Have I let them down? What can I do to make them feel better? Should I take more responsibility for the unfulfilled longing in their hearts? They are depressed, dissatisfied, hopeless, and in despair: Surely this is somehow traceable back to me, right? I've failed somehow, right? If I do not fix this situation, I will be discarded, abandoned, neglected, or abused. I just know it. I must act quickly."

As a little one yearning for some degree of empathic connection, we're willing to do just about *anything* to receive even a limited amount of attention, mirroring, and affection. We'll open certain parts of ourselves and close others; pretend to feel a certain way and disavow what we're actually experiencing; disown parts of ourselves and unnaturally cultivate others, all in the hopes of keeping the bond alive. We'll do whatever it takes if there is even a glimmer of a hope of being seen, being met, being touched, being loved. "Just tell me what to do, and I'll do it. Even if you don't tell me, I'll try to figure it out. Don't worry, I'm here. I'll figure out what you need and sacrifice myself on whatever altar necessary in order to fill the black hole within you. Even if it creates deep wounding and pain for me, don't worry. I'm here."

To allow in the reality of what happened for many of us as young children in this way is not easy. It can be quite painful and even traumatic, but it is a profound act of self-care to begin to untangle the web. Illuminating and reorganizing the tentacles of this template can go a long way in healing chronic feelings of shame and unworthiness. We begin to differentiate our worth as a person from the moods, suffering, struggle, and unlived life of another. To do this, we must withdraw the projection of our own worth from the other and relocate it inside ourselves, which is no easy task. It requires that we turn back toward all parts of ourselves and associated feelings from which we previously split off to maintain the tie with the caretaker—to allow these emotions and aspects of our personalities a safe haven to return to, where we can warm them, listen to them, hold them, and welcome them back home, slowly and safely at a pace that is provocative but not overwhelming.

Through this process of disentangling, we might come to truly know the difference between caring for another from a place of true compassion and reenacting earlier pathways of self-abandonment. Although it might seem obvious, this discernment requires deepening awareness and practice, especially in the subtler forms of re-creating this self-abandonment in real time. Helping, caring for, and being there for another are noble acts, especially when undertaken without enactment of earlier, less healthy relational configurations. Learning to recognize and act from true compassion, toward ourselves and others, is a great gift we can offer this world. To do this, we must train ourselves to work with activated emotional states when they arise; to turn back toward ourselves; and to provide the empathy, compassion, and holding that for many was not available in earlier times.

In ways we might never have expected, even the most difficult experiences of loss, deflation, and disappointment carry a certain intelligence and soul if we can tend to them in a new way. We discover the creativity in the cycle of death and rebirth not by abandoning the "death" aspect of the spiral too quickly but by honoring the full spectrum. By training ourselves to validate, honor, and learn from the inevitable inner and outer transitions we face, we provide sanctuary for new light to emerge and new vision to enter our lives. Because so many of our difficult thoughts and feelings arise from the experience of loss, by learning to navigate these times of transition and change with more curiosity, awareness, and kindness, we can use even these challenging experiences to help come closer to and befriend ourselves in those moments we truly need ourselves more than ever.

5

SHIFTING OUR
CENTER OF GRAVITY

*Approaching the Idea of "Integration"
with Fresh Vision*

IN THIS CHAPTER, WE'LL TAKE a reimagined look at the concept of "integration" and what it might mean in an embodied and personal way, and how our "center of gravity" can begin to shift as our inquiry unfolds. We'll go through a meditation on integration that will invite us into an exploration of multiple layers of our experience, with the intention of including the full range of our humanness in our practice. We'll explore the image of the alchemical *separatio* (separation) and its critical role in transformation and healing, along with the importance of this process to the larger aim of befriending ourselves in difficult times. Although "separation" is often spoken of pejoratively in contemporary spirituality, where we find an emphasis on unity and oneness, we are invited to *also* embrace the separate and the multiple as dignified aspects of psyche, as authentic and important dimensions and expressions of our human experience, with an integral approach to spiritual and psychological growth.

As we deepen in our capacity to befriend all parts of ourselves—including the most triggering thoughts, feelings, and sensations—we might notice our center of gravity beginning to shift. It's not so much that the limiting beliefs, disturbing emotions, and habitual ways of perceiving have stopped or even lessened, necessarily, but that they come and go in the context of a much larger space. As I've mentioned, it is common to conclude that the presence of difficult experience is clear evidence that we are stunted in our growth, doing it wrong, lost, neurotic, or horribly unawakened. Upon investigation, however, we might discover that the mere *appearance* of this material is not problematic or the primary cause of our struggle. Rather, our relationship with the material and disconnection with the space in which it is arising and unfolding is the issue. In alchemical language, there is always a container (*vas hermeticum*) in which the thoughts, feelings, emotions, memories, and images appear and dissolve. The invitation, from this perspective, is not to get rid of unwanted material but to heat it up in the vessel and allow it to be transmuted into its essence. The fire that produces this heat comes from our curiosity, interest, care, and love, for the manifestations of psyche, for the truth, and by way of our aspiration to no longer abandon ourselves.

In this new environment, where we start to notice this shift, we find ourselves in close, intimate contact with the emotional world, with thoughts and feelings we have historically repressed, acted out, or become flooded by. But now we are not so close that we fuse or fall into them, where we drown and become completely caught in our experience. In exploring the alchemical middle territory of which I spoke earlier, we no longer need the feelings to go away but want to know them more fully, to infuse them with curiosity, warmth, and presence. More than anything, we are drawn to call off the war—to step off the battlefield, for there are no more enemies left. We are no longer willing to turn away from our feeling and sensitivity, to attack our own vulnerability, to bail out of our bodies, or to meet the inner world with violence and aggression. Even if we do not *like* what appears, we begin to sense that it, too, has a place in the larger inner ecology of what we are, somehow intelligently arising here as part of our work and our art.

The sense of unworthiness, the panic in the belly, the avalanche-like rage, the deeply embedded conviction that there is something wrong with us can appear. The feeling of shame, the ruminations of despair, the constriction in the throat, the loneliness in the heart—saturated with intelligence and information, soaked with some sort of sacred knowledge that yearns to be integrated—might appear. Underneath the thoughts, feelings, and bodily sensations, we might come to discover a raw, tender, shaky core. It's so alive there, a womb of creativity, but not quite knowable in the ordinary sense. To mine this hidden gold, we have to continue to discover new ways of befriending our experience, to set aside old ideas about what it means to have an emotion, to think more creatively, and to imagine in new ways.

REIMAGINING THE IDEA OF INTEGRATION

We hear a lot about "integration" and how essential it is on the path of awakening, healing, and psychological transformation, but the word is often thrown around without any clear sense of what we're referring to. What would it actually look and feel like to "integrate" an aspect of our experience, a difficult feeling or emotion, our personality—to "be" an integrated person? We have an image or idea of what the word points to that helps us to speak about it, but as with so many of these concepts, we must take the time to unpack what we mean and revision these ideas to keep them relevant and alive.

The way I tend to use the word is not with regard to some final end state in which we "integrate" our personality or our shadow but, more pragmatically, means we weave together the various layers and dimensions of our lived experience—thoughts, feelings, sensations, impulses, and images. In the field of interpersonal neurobiology, for example, this idea is expressed as *linking together differentiated elements in a system,* said to foster neural, psychic, and relational health.[1] Analogously, in a way we might not expect from such an ancient and diverse tradition, the alchemists remind us that we cannot unite that which has not first been separated.[2] Therefore, the process of separation (*separatio*) is essential, in which the material is differentiated (broken down into its component parts) so that it is approachable, workable, and available for the various alchemical operations.

The alchemical process is parallel to inner work, in which we must differentiate abstract and generalized conditions such as anxiety, depression, sadness, rage, jealousy, and so forth into specific and particularized, separated parts so that we are able to work directly with the individualized components of our lived experience. For example, it is difficult, if not impossible, to work effectively, imaginatively, and creatively with a generalized abstraction such as "depression," a concept that appears differently for each of us across the layers of experience in the form of specific core beliefs, memories, images, moods, emotional tones, felt senses, and behavioral impulses. From this perspective, there is no one thing called "depression" but a unique assemblage of lived, embodied experience we must differentiate to tend to this painful condition in a skillful and compassionate way.

This process of differentiation, by way of the alchemical *separatio* and our own mindful awareness, is equally critical to that of linkage, or the alchemical *coagulatio*, in which the material moves back into unity from a separated state to one of togetherness. Although the experience of "oneness" is often privileged in the realms of spirituality, I would like to invite you to consider the possibility that the experience of multiplicity is just as holy, as valid, and as "spiritual." In a more poetic way, God itself has no bias toward unity or multiplicity, oneness or differentiation, but rather expresses itself through each of these perspectives to disclose one of its qualities or fragrances. We need not take sides but only enter into communion with each of these energies from perspectives of curiosity, interest, passion, and warmth. Interestingly, the subtitle to Jung's alchemical opus *Mysterium Coniunctionis* is "An inquiry into the separation *and* synthesis of psychic opposites in alchemy," reflecting the importance of *both* processes in the journey of transformation, healing, and individuation.[3]

TRAUMA, INTEGRATION, AND HEALING

Before we go too far into integration, it's important to address one of the common ways in which the term is used (along with the word "healing") that has led to some confusion. It is essential that we reenvision words such as "integration" and "healing," for they can so easily lose their meaning, magic, and life force. Before we know it, these concepts can become further tools of shame, blame, and self-abandonment. We must breathe life back into these ideas in an imaginative, grounded, and creative way.

Often what people mean by "integrating" or "healing" trauma is that one day we will "get over it," "transcend" it, "outgrow" it, meditate it away, or otherwise purge it from our psychic-emotional-somatic being. As if the trauma were some sort of actual "thing" that exists inside of us, a common view is that we can get in there and remove it through some sort of procedure. In my experience, this view of trauma is in large part inaccurate, aggressive, misguided, and at times even dangerous and violent. We will never "get over" some things that happen to us, and this would not even be an appropriate goal or lens to use in approaching the sacredness of human experience.

But if what we mean by "integration" is discovering a place inside where we can hold and contain our experience, make sense of what happened in new ways, bring together and tend to the shards of dissociation, and discover deeper meaning, then these concepts can come alive again. Slowly, over time, we can begin to bear that which has been unbearable, providing sanctuary and safe passage for the pieces of the broken self to reorganize.

As we train ourselves to reinhabit our bodies even in the face of profoundly disturbing experience, we can begin to weave a more "integrated" narrative of our lives, reauthoring the sacred story of who we are, what has happened to us, and how we are being called into a future not yet known. We can gather the pieces and begin to trust in the validity of our experience again.

The goal, then, is not some fixed, "cured" state in which we have successfully purged an aspect of our experience from what we are, as if it were some wretched foreign substance. Rather, the invitation is to find a larger home for it within us. Slowly, we can allow what has become frozen and solidified to thaw and become flexible. Perhaps, when all is said and done, self-love will soften the wounds of the body and the heart, for they will never unwind in an environment of abandonment and aggression. It's just not safe or majestic enough there.

In this way, perhaps we can salvage the concepts of "integration" and "healing," at least for today, reenvisioning and reenchanting them with the force of an uncompromising and unapologetic compassion, slowness, patience, and care of the soul, as we open into the mystery together.

ALCHEMICAL INTEGRATION

Through the alchemical process of *separatio*, we differentiate the material we are working with, in this case our various layers of here-and-now experience, so that we can attend to each layer on its own. If we try to approach our inner world all at once, we can become overwhelmed and not sure where or how to start. How do I deal with this depression, this anxiety, this heartbreak, this hopelessness? These huge psychological concepts are general and abstract and cannot be approached until they are first broken down into their component parts, into bite-sized pieces of immediate, lived experience. Although it is difficult to wrap our minds around and approach "depression," it *is* possible to tend to specific, repetitive thoughts that life isn't worth living, a blackened empty hole in the heart, a feeling of nausea in the belly, or an impulse to hide so that no one can see us. In this sense, there is no such thing as "depression" in the abstract. We can't work with that. It's too vague, too monstrous, too overwhelming, too theoretical, too much. We can't find it in the vessel, grab ahold of it, and heat it. Therefore we cannot come to know its qualities, essences, and meanings. It's just too conceptual, too clinical, too experience-distant. From an alchemical perspective, the way we make "depression" experience-close is to first separate out the component parts into smaller, more precise, more manageable pieces that we can then warm with the fire of curiosity, awareness, and compassion.

Not only must we separate the layers from each other—core beliefs from emotions from sensations from impulses and so forth—but also we must "separate" ourselves from the material so we can gain some perspective on it, are not overly identified with it, and can reflect *on* it without becoming fused *with* it. Often, we remain embedded and enmeshed within our experience, not realizing that thoughts and feelings come and go and are not objective "facts" merely because they appear. Just because we think or feel something does not mean it is an accurate reflection of reality. Although this assertion might seem obvious on the surface, to allow in the implications of its experiential realization can be life changing.

This capacity to reflect upon our experience—in analytic literature referred to as "mentalizing"—is essential on the path of healing and transformation.[4] We can distinguish this capacity of reflection upon the *content* of our experience from meditative awareness, which is not as focused upon the content but rather upon the *nature* of any arising thought, feeling, or emotion or upon the *context* in which it arises and passes. In this way, psychological reflection is concerned with unpacking our immediate experience and exploring its qualities, implicit and relational meanings, historical associations, why it has come, what it needs, and where it is leading us. We'll look at these two modes of inquiry—content and context—in more detail in chapter 6.

We all know what it's like to step back and reflect on a difficult situation in our lives, or a feeling, or a limited belief we have about ourselves or another. We also know what it's like to merge with the experience, lose perspective, and fall into it, unable to find any space between ourselves and the challenging material that has come in a moment of activation. At times, before we know it, we are completely identified with the thought or feeling, have fused with it, equated it with objective reality, and no longer see it as temporary, passing experience. In this state of embeddedness, it is not possible to engage with the material with clear perception because we are caught within it. It takes practice to separate from charged inner experience so that we can gain perspective and reflect upon it while not separating so much that we move into dissociation, denial, or disconnection. We must discover the nature of this middle territory for ourselves, what it feels like in our bodies and minds, in the fire of our own direct experience. The invitation is to come close but not *so* close that we merge with the thought or feeling and lose the ground underneath us. It's a delicate balance, somewhat like learning how to use the pedal and clutch together while driving; at first it can feel awkward and clunky, but over time, with practice, it can become second nature.

SEPARATING THE LAYERS OF OUR EXPERIENCE

To undertake this process, it can be helpful to have some basic skills in mindfulness that help us to apprehend the moment-to-moment unfolding of our present experience, nonjudgmentally and in an environment of spaciousness and warmth. Although the awareness or clarity side of mindfulness is often most emphasized—and in some sense, this is for good reason—in my experience it is equally (if at times, not more important) to underscore bringing acceptance and compassion to what we experience. What this looks like for each of us will be different, and we must discover for ourselves what it would mean to "be kind" to a painful feeling, belief about ourselves, or sensation in the body. How would we "open our hearts" to an emotion, image, or series of repetitive thoughts? It can seem a bit abstract at first, but over time we can come to an experiential understanding of what it would be like in any given moment to infuse our present experience—even incredibly intense and challenging experience—with kindness. In other words, the practice becomes as much a "heart" practice as one of increasing clarity and awareness.

During a moment of activation, it can seem as if we are drowning, as if an enemy were coming at us from the outside. Slowing down and beginning to differentiate the layers can help convert the experience into "bite-sized" pieces, more approachable than an undifferentiated mass of struggle and confusion. The alchemists referred to this unworkable, undefinable, unmanageable nature of inner process as a *massa confusa,* a "confused mass," difficult to relate to and handle.[5] We cannot work with it directly but must apply the proper heat (awareness and love) so that it can be broken down into its component parts, separating them out so we can attend to each in turn. This process of differentiating previously linked aspects of our experience allows us to isolate the *prima materia,* the specific substance that wants attention *now,* focusing us on what most needs tending in our lives in *this* moment. This differentiating process doesn't happen in some abstract, generalized way distant to our experience but in close and intimate, concrete, and specific ways.

If we attempt to relate to our experience as *massa confusa,* we will likely get overwhelmed, flooded, and lost. At that point we seem to have no recourse but to fall back into historical, conditioned strategies to take us out of the fire and back to safe ground. It's as if there's a monster we're being asked to confront, some huge entity that has come into our psychic space, and we have no perspective from which to engage it. There is no space between us and it, no possibility of standing back and making sense of this material in our lives; instead, it's as if we are embedded within it in a way that can feel claustrophobic. Whether the monster takes form as rage, shame, depression, jealousy, fear, numbness, or confusion, there's a sense that it's just not quite workable; we can't relate to it in its current form.

THE IMPORTANCE OF SEPARATION *AND* SYNTHESIS

First, as always, we must recognize that we have become hooked into and embedded within our experience and have lost contact with the spacious awareness in which the cascading thoughts, feelings, and sensations are coming and going. Rather than react to this recognition with shame, blame, and self-attack ("There I go again, I'm never going to get it right, I've failed again," etc.), we can be grateful that enough awareness has been constellated to allow us to slow down and open to the possibility to befriend our experience in a new way. This one moment of recognition cuts into billions of prior moments of repression, rejection, resistance, and unconsciousness. A moment of grace, insight, self-compassion, and self-care. Yes, it might appear that a monster has arrived, the *massa confusa* in one of its infinite forms, but the veil has pulled back a bit. With clear seeing, attunement, and kindness, we step back and reflect, gather some perspective, and catch ourselves before we totally fall into old patterns. And even if we've already fallen down the rabbit hole, we can use this awareness, this pause, this compassion to step back out. From this ground of recognition, slowing down and seeing that we've been caught or hooked, we realize some material is asking to be tended to, heated up, embraced, and befriended.

This brings us back to the processes of separation *and* synthesis and the subtitle of Jung's major opus, "An Inquiry into the Separation and Synthesis of Psychic Opposites in Alchemy." As indicated by Jung's subtitle, these two concepts are useful metaphors as we imagine what a process of "integration" might entail. Both are required and essential as part of any integrative process. There can be no integration without conscious tending to each; one without the other does not allow for a complete integration to occur.

One of the phrases often put forth as a summary of alchemical work is *solve et coagula*, dissolve and coagulate.[6] Dissolve/coagulate, separate/synthesize, differentiate/link—these are some of the core images that point to this process of recognizing, slowing down, and exploring the material that comes in charged emotional moments. As part of this exploration, we break up the mass of confusion into its component parts, only to relink them at a later moment after we've met and attended to each on their own, synthesizing our experience in an integrative way that reveals the workability of even our most challenging thoughts, feelings, impulses, and sensations.

In order to accomplish this, exploring that which most needs our attention in a given here-and-now moment, we cycle through the different layers of our experience, differentiating the "confused mass" into bite-sized pieces to which we can tend with greater awareness, perspective, and compassion. We're no longer attempting to work with "sadness," "anxiety," "depression," or "jealousy" per se—generalized, abstract, clinical concepts—but with present, embodied experience, unique to us in *this* moment, particularized, and concrete. We can begin with whatever layer is calling our attention, with no particular agenda, though ensuring that at some point during our inquiry we touch on each of the four primary areas: mood, belief, sensation, and impulse. By doing so, we weave a tapestry of the here and now, separating the individual components and then allowing them to come back together in a way that honors the multiplicity—as well as the oneness—of our lived experience. This linking of differentiated aspects is the essence of integration, or in Jung's language, the synthesizing of separated parts.[7]

A MEDITATION ON INTEGRATION

Find a place where you can be alone and undisturbed for fifteen or twenty minutes (you can also do this meditation over the course of two to three minutes after you develop some experience with it). Allow yourself to relax as deeply as you're able while at the same time being as aware as you can of what is happening inside and around you, with your senses open and curious. You can do this meditation with eyes open or closed. It might be helpful to experiment with both.

1. **First, slow down and fully arrive in this moment.** Take a few slow and deep breaths; feel your feet or bottom on the ground and the earth supporting you. You are *already* held by something larger, without having to deserve it, change first, shift, transform, or heal. Allow yourself to feel held. It is causeless. Give yourself to this moment.

   This meditation is an embodied practice, meaning it is important that your body be a part of the meditation, in each phase. Use your awareness and your breath to stay attuned to your body as you go through each of the steps, remembering that body awareness is a critical aspect to integration but often left out or underemphasized in a lot of psychological and spiritual practices.

2. **Mood.** Start by bringing your attention to the overall mood you are experiencing. Open your senses and allow yourself to connect with all the subtleties of the mood—its texture, color, and fragrance. How are you feeling in this moment? What is alive within you? What is the overall felt sense of the environment, inside and around you? Are you aware of any emotions? See if

you can touch this global mood without using any words to describe it, at least at first.

After you have made a connection with the emotional tone present, play with a word or two that describes your mood, spontaneously and flexibly allowing language to mingle with the felt sense but not allowing words and concepts to overtake your primary connection with the mood itself. Rest your awareness in the core of the feeling and observe as it moves, dances, unfolds, and changes. Allow the emotion or mood the space to express itself as best you are able.

3. **Belief.** After you're attuned to the general mood present—the overall felt sense of your immediate experience—open your awareness and allow it to fill and touch and expand into the entire space you are in, no longer focusing on the mood per se, while at the same time perfectly open to return to it should it ask for more specified attention.

In moments of activation (but not limited to these times only), when we are triggered or thrown off center, one or two core beliefs usually underlie the mood, are woven into the feeling, or are otherwise related to the overall emotional tone in some way. You might experience these beliefs as "supporting" the mood or vice versa. Allow yourself to remain in a state of not knowing about this; there's no need to figure it out or resolve which comes first. Stay curious and open.

What core beliefs have accompanied you for so long, forming the lenses through which you see and imagine yourself, having journeyed with you as a kindred traveler? To uncover these essential narratives and images, ask yourself: "When I am feeling sad, jealous, hopeless, ashamed, confused, angry, scared, bored, unsafe, flat, or [insert feeling/mood here], what do I *believe* about myself, about others, about the world? What core beliefs are circling when I am activated in this way? What habitual thoughts and fundamental perceptions seem to underlie these emotional states?

For example, if I'm feeling shame or despair, do I believe that there is something fundamentally wrong with me, that I am unlovable, that I have failed, that no one will ever want to get close to me, that no one will ever understand me, or that I'm not okay as I am? Do I believe that the world is unsafe, that I can't depend on another, or that others are out to get me?

Allow the beliefs to present themselves—including any accompanying images, memories, fantasies, or further feelings—without any sense that they need to be changed, transformed, or healed. Provide a safe place for the beliefs to reveal themselves. It can help to write them down if you feel drawn to do so.

For the purposes of this meditation, we are not working to change these beliefs or replace them with others but only to shine a light into and through them with as much awareness, presence, and compassion as we are able—to illuminate the lenses through which we have come to perceive ourselves, others, and the world.

4. **Sensation.** After you've identified the global mood or overall emotional quality—and touched and named any associated core beliefs—move more deeply into your body. The level of raw sensation is unfamiliar to many. Although most of us are clear as to how to identify a thought, feeling, or impulse to act, the sensations alive in our bodies are not quite as accessible or obvious, at least not at first. It can take some practice to connect with sensations—to feel the heat, pressure, constriction, flow, light, dark, cold, tension, speed, holes, expansion, contraction, space, and

pulsation in various parts of our bodies. So much information in our bodies is profoundly relevant to our journeys of healing and transformation, but many of us must train ourselves to attune to this layer of experience.

As a mode of focus, for some it can be helpful to pay particular attention to what is happening in their bellies, hearts, and throats because much of our emotional and psychic material is stored in these three areas. But this is only a guideline. It is important to scan through your entire body to discover and attune to what is most wanting and needing attention.

Take a moment and sweep your awareness (and kindness) through your body, becoming curious and open to whatever raw sensations are coursing through. Allow your awareness to focus on an area where your attention is drawn, and just practice staying with the sensation, observing its qualities and how it moves and expresses itself. Infuse the sensation with breath, awareness, compassion, and warmth. No need to try to understand, transform, shift, or heal any of the sensations but only to befriend yourself at deeper and deeper levels.

5. **Impulse.** Often, when we are triggered or the nervous system is aroused, we will experience a variety of impulses to take some sort of action, usually with the intention of getting us out of feelings and states of vulnerability, which feel unsafe or otherwise unmanageable. We want to discharge the intense, disturbing, and claustrophobic energy, usually as quickly as possible.

As a simple example, we might notice an impulse to run to the refrigerator to find some food, even though we are not actually hungry, but we feel drawn to fill a certain emptiness in the belly or heart. Or we might notice an urgent impulse to send our partner or friend a text during an argument when we are upset, or to send an email to a colleague not out of a sense of grounded presence but to avoid some emotional experience that feels unworkable and potentially overwhelming. Or we might have the impulse to turn on the television, have a drink, or scroll through Facebook. We each have our characteristic ways of cutting into an uncomfortable or uncertain moment with a particular set of activities.

When we feel sad, jealous, hopeless, or enraged—aware of a flood of ruminative thoughts, beliefs, and sensations in the body—we're invited to pay careful attention to the habitual and addictive behaviors in which we engage (or are drawn to engage, but maybe haven't yet initiated) to bring immediate relief to ourselves. It is natural to want to soothe ourselves during stressful and challenging times; however, addictive and automatic actions, although perhaps helpful for a few moments, tend to generate more struggle and suffering over time, a reality most of us have learned the hard way.

In a moment of activation, what is your go-to behavior? What do you feel drawn to *do*? In what ways do you abandon yourself and your immediate experience in the face of powerful, difficult emotions? What would it be like to notice the impulse to take action and, instead of following it right away, to bring awareness, compassion, and kindness to yourself, to care for yourself in a new way, to first see what wants to be met in this charged moment? Even for only a few seconds, open to sitting in this challenging, hot, sticky, claustrophobic middle territory, where you might be burning to take action, to somehow escape the intensity and vulnerability of the moment.

6. **Integration.** Finally, let go of tending to any individual layer of experience, open your awareness, and allow yourself to connect with all the layers *at once*—mood, sensation, belief, impulse.

Don't *think* about the layers, just relax into the alive field of energy that you are. Feel how the layers dance and interpenetrate with each other, with mood triggering core beliefs, generating sensations in the body, leading to impulses to move into action, constellating more thinking, leading to more emotion, and so forth.

At times, a mood might most get your attention, so you start there; at other times, a sensation in the body, an image, a memory, or repetitive thinking around a particular theme. It's important to note that any session of inquiry will always be unique and might never conform to any particular set of instructions, including these. Like the alchemist in search of the ever-elusive *prima materia*, allow the "primary material" of your own experience in the moment to guide you. For example, you might notice the mood leading to an awareness of a limiting belief, a sensation in the body that reveals a core emotional vulnerability, an image underlying the various thoughts and feelings that wants to be tended to. The embodied experience of one emotion might lead to another, previously hidden feeling. Trust your psyche to reveal to you what is most alive and relevant in the miracle of the here and now, knowing that the unfolding of the material in the vessel has its own intelligence and order.

Allow the separated layers to link, play off and with each other, and rest in attunement with the true miracle of the human experience—all the subtlety, nuance, and magic, really, of what it means to be alive. Pay careful attention to how the layers of experience that have been differentiated and separated come together in union, integrating in the spontaneous flow of life.

You can practice this meditation during times of stress and activation or when nothing in particular is going on, which can also be interesting and revealing. As you become more familiar with the practice, you might discover that it takes only a minute or two to go through it, or you could take thirty or forty-five minutes to tend to the different levels if you have extra time and inclination. Even if you are busy, you can usually find three to five minutes to check in with yourself and start to build the neural foundation and resources that will support whatever inner work you are most drawn to.

By first differentiating the various layers and then bringing them together, we foster integration. We separate, then synthesize— *solve et coagula*—differentiate, then link. Over time, as you practice this meditation, you might discover a natural spaciousness in your experience, even during difficult times. It is a practice of lovingkindness, self-discovery, and wisdom and provides a simple foundation of insight and nourishing self-care.

THE ONLY WAY OUT IS THROUGH

Although there might be a certain excitement about this opening to a new world, it is important that we create a home for the visitors of trepidation, fear, and ambivalence—to offer a great feast where all the figures can come. If we deny these entry out of some belief in their invalidity, they *will* find other ways to emerge, leaking into and out of our bodies, relationships, work, and dreams. The unwanted ones are not enemies, obstacles, or obfuscations but come as light in disguise.

It is not always easy to access thoughts, feelings, images, and sensations, especially those previously disavowed or otherwise dwelling outside conscious awareness. Tending to material that has found its way into the shadow—charged psychic states such as fear, vulnerability, and shame—is essential on any path of healing, for by way of access and articulation we can make sense of and integrate the material.

Despite the cliché, it does seem the only way out is through, if we are interested in aliveness rather than mere symptom reduction (which of course is also a valid and honorable outcome and goal). The relational context, for some, provides an environment in which we can access, articulate, and make sense of our experience *with another*.[8] Therapeutically as well as through the practice of mindful inquiry, it is possible, over time, to transform early organizations of experience that arose from developmental trauma, consistent empathic failure, and insecure attachment. The point here is that solo work *and* relational work are both important and offer different portals and passageways into the mystery.

The basic idea is that the more profound and deeply embedded the trauma, the more helpful relationship will be to bring forth and embody lasting transformation and healing. Although there are always exceptions, in my experience this is a general rule that almost always bears out in practice. Most of us cannot meditate our trauma away. This doesn't mean there is something problematic or lacking in our meditative practices but that for many, meditation is not capable of working with the entire spectrum because no singular method or approach can do that.

When I speak about the importance of relationship and making the journey with another, I am not referring only to a formal therapeutic relationship but to any relationship emotionally significant to us—a friend, a lover, a family member, a coworker, or even a stranger or inspiring figure from literature, myth, film, or spiritual tradition. Also, an animal-friend or personified aspect of the natural world can be the other. Even God himself or herself can be an attachment figure—most important is the quality of *otherness* that we touch in relationship with a being whom we can feel, who cares about us and joins us in the relational field, where we can be together.

BE A FRIEND TO YOURSELF

The next time you find yourself cycling in self-attack—disconnected and spinning in shame, blame, and complaint—notice what is happening, and slow down. Feel your feet on the earth. Breathe deeply from your lower belly. Return to your senses in the here and now. The sounds. The sights. The smells. The tastes. Touch something. Allow yourself to be touched by what has arrived.

Come out of the sticky, seductive story line for just a moment and send awareness into the center of the vulnerable, tender, raw life surging to be held. Go slowly, pushing yourself a bit, testing your window of tolerance but taking care not to spiral outside it into overwhelm. Cut through the momentum of self-abandonment and descend into the core. Make the journey out of self-aggression and into the slower circuitry of curiosity, attunement, and space.

Stay close. Be a friend to yourself. Provide sanctuary and safe passage for the visitors to be illuminated and held, for in a moment of activation you need yourself more than ever. Although the temptation is to turn from the shaky center, it is an act of love to step off the battlefield and tend to the fire with the cooling waters of lovingkindness. Your torso is aglow with important data required for the way ahead and is a portal of life and creativity.

As you give yourself this gift of radical self-compassion, presence, and slow spacious awareness, you can ask: What is it that I need right now? What is most needing to be met and held? What have I abandoned in myself? What is being asked to be touched, to be heard, to be felt? Can I breathe into what has come, not as an obstacle to transcend but as an ally of the depths? How can I truly *listen* in a new way?

As you slow down and turn back home, seeds of empathy are planted in your nervous system, watered with new forms of self-care as compassion pathways find their grooves and are brought alive. Suddenly there is so much space. Breath where none was to be found. You are already held by something vast.

Through this aspiration to no longer abandon yourself, you come back into your power, grounded and embodied in the reality and perception of the warrior, a warrior of love who has come here not only to heal yourself but as a vessel of presence and transmutation for all beings.

Take a moment before moving on to the next chapter to rest and allow yourself to open to your immediate experience. Listen to the sounds around you, feel your feelings, sense your sensations, and *see* what is in front of and inside of you. Remember that you can return to this chapter's meditation at any time, even if you have only a few minutes while on the train, in line at the grocery store, on a break at work, or waiting for an appointment.

As we learn to tend to and infuse each layer of our experience with newfound attention, awareness, and warmth, trust in the workability of our lives naturally arises as well as the courage and curiosity to go deeper, confident that we can meet ourselves and our world in a new way.

6

THE GREAT DANCE OF
BEING AND BECOMING

MANY PEOPLE HAVE EXPERIENCED THE POWER of the present moment; accepting what is; calling off the war with reality; and meeting immediate experience with mindful, nonjudgmental presence and compassion. One of the most common spiritual adages of the past few decades has encouraged us to spend more time *being* and less time *doing*, approaching life in a way oriented in freedom from unnecessary suffering and struggle. There is a lot of wisdom in living our lives in the here and now and not losing contact with the essential beingness eternally present. As always, though, it is important to inquire as deeply as possible into these matters to mine the complexity, nuance, and creativity in the contradictions and multiple perspectives. As profound as the teaching to "live in the present moment" might be, we cannot reduce the entirety of the human journey to a catchphrase or one particular method or approach. The heart is just too vast, too majestic, too unique, too precious.

When a challenging core belief, emotion, or life situation arrives, do we accept it and flood it with present-centered, compassionate awareness? Do we allow it to be what it is, to dance and play and spin and twirl, only to dissolve yet again back into the great natural perfection? Or do we engage with the material more actively and enter into relationship—get messy, burn with it, ask it why it has come, and explore its meaning and purpose?

Do we return to the present moment, disidentifying with the passing thoughts, feelings, and sensations, or do we dive *into* them, following the psychic thread to access the wisdom buried in the content itself, not just in its essential nature? *Being* asks that we apprehend and attune to the *context* (or spacious background field) in which all our experience arises, whereas *becoming* wants us to know the *content* itself with more and more intimacy, engaging in a journey with the material in an unfolding process in time.

From the perspective of the meditator or yogi, you might imagine that she or he rests in pure consciousness, in unconditioned awareness, not caught up in the infinite forms that appear but rather dwelling in the natural perfection of the moment. Here, they return over and over to this background field, not becoming tangled in the endless stream of experience. In contrast, from the perspective of the alchemist, you might imagine that he or she delves into the mess of the material, fully hands on with senses open and engaged, entering the imaginal world with a longing for communion and exploration, wanting to know everything possible about the material—its color, fragrance, and essence—even its "mood," the way *it* perceives and all of its qualities, contours, and textures. Remember, for the alchemist—and for each of us as we engage our lives alchemically—the "material" of our lives is intelligent, alive, and has its own integrity, voice, and even subjectivity. We must enter into our experience in a curious, imaginal way to unlock these mysteries and mine the wisdom within us. This is something each of us can do, and it is my primary purpose in this book to offer pathways, portals, and varied invitations into the richness of this inner discovery.

Generally speaking, tending to the context or ground of our experience but not explicitly exploring the content, its qualities, and meanings is the invitation from the meditative traditions, whereas unpacking, unfolding, and embracing the content itself and the potential wisdom it contains is that of the alchemical or depth psychological approaches. How these two lenses and streams intersect, interact, contradict, and support each other are among the topics we'll explore together in this chapter, with the underlying idea that including *both* perspectives will allow us to befriend ourselves at the deepest levels and reveal a healing space that is creative, transformative, and even beautiful in its landscape.

How will we ever come to terms with the teachings on acceptance when there is a part of us that genuinely wishes for things to change? It can seem like such a contradiction at times: "I hear that I'm supposed to just accept what arises, and that is the key to lasting freedom, happiness, and peace. But the truth is that I *don't* accept it. If I'm being fully honest with myself, I want some things in my life to change. I want to transform and heal and grow and improve certain parts of myself and my life." It's such an honest and human confession and deserves not judgment and shame but validation. The art of facilitating a dialogue between these two voices and their associated images, feelings, impulses, and behaviors is rich terrain for us to include as part of our inquiry, without any fantasy that the goal is to achieve some sort of resolution. The creative, quantum flow of aliveness we long for will never be found in some project of sorting it all out but only in turning toward the intelligence of the contradiction itself, which is saturated with life.

Being and becoming. Acceptance and change. Transformation and rest. Yin and yang. These are the great archetypal energies we meet when we do this work. As with all psychic opposites, they will never be wrapped up into some neat, tidy package in which we can find resolution, for they are too alive. *We can't resolve an archetype.* We just can't pin them down into some preprogrammed philosophy of life, even if doing so might (temporarily) alleviate some of the uncertainty and anxiety. In tending to the apparent contradictions, we face a conundrum: "Oh, I see, I should just accept everything exactly the way it is. That is the way to peace. Any urge to improve my sense of self or life situation is clear evidence I have fallen off the path. I should return to presence and call off the search." The other extreme is to spend nearly all our precious life energy trying to grow and expand who we are and to change the circumstances of our lives, relationships, and inner experience. We engage in what can appear to be an unending project and become utterly exhausted over time. How to navigate this?

The invitation, as with all contradictory energies, is into the rich, unknown middle territory, alive with information and potentiality. Although we will never be able to *resolve* the mystery of yin and yang, we can begin to facilitate a *dialogue* between them, to cultivate an attitude of play and dance as we weave in and out of the poles, allowing a new, "third" position to emerge.[1] This new emergent is not some homogenized or watered-down compromise but saturated with the intelligence and creativity of multiple perspectives, bringing conscious attitudes and unconscious content together in the immediacy of now, revealing a way forward that transcends previous ways of thinking, perceiving, and being.

But how do we find a way through these seemingly opposite energies in our lived experience? Although the meditatively oriented approaches ask us to accept things as they are, set aside the dream of a "future moment," and return to immediacy, other forms of inquiry encourage us to work diligently and creatively to heal and transform ourselves, to actively participate in the process of transmutation as it occurs within the vessel of our lives. We can feel the wisdom from both sides, but how do we reconcile what appears to be two different worlds? How can we simultaneously honor the authentic longing to change our lives with the truth we've discovered when staying in the present and setting aside our need to improve our immediate experience? It's almost as if we must become two different people (or three or four) to make any sense of all this and honor the entirety of what we are.

It's not so much that we need to "become" multiple people but to recognize that multiple people already exist within us; in this sense psyche itself *is* multiple.[2] There is no singular, permanent, solid, continuous, fixed "voice" within us that "is" the psyche or "the" personality. In postmodern analytic language, the self is a construction that arises intersubjectively and relationally, not one single entity that serves as command central for the personality, existing separately and apart from the context in which the sense of self arises. We find this relative nature of the self echoed as well in many of the contemplative traditions, for example in the various schools of Buddhism. Rather than pointing to some rigid metaphysical conclusion that there "is" no self, the Mahayana Buddhist teaching of "two truths" acknowledges the relative nature of the self, the reality that most of us *experience* a sense of self even while questioning its ultimate status. In a similar way, for Jung and the analytical psychologists, the goal isn't to "get rid of" the ego but to relativize it—to allow it to take its place in psyche as one figure or image among many.

Parts of us yearn for rest, acceptance, and pure being, whereas others have little or no interest in those states and are called instead to engage in the organic process of becoming, over time, exploring and experimenting with transformation. How do we validate both? How do we listen to and honor each of the voices without going crazy? It's an important question and a critical aspect of any full-spectrum inquiry. Somehow, we must cultivate the capacity to embrace these contradictions and flexibly engage both without any fantasy that we're going to one day feel only one way about these matters or that one is "right" and the other "wrong" and so forth. Rather than getting into some emotional battle in which we feel like we need to take sides, we become more and more psychically supple and creative, privileging *being* at one moment only to shift to *becoming* in another, without any sense that we will conceptually come to terms with these two great energies and movements in consciousness. Over time, we begin to discover that the aliveness and creativity are within the core of the apparent contradictions themselves rather than in their resolution.

At times, rest and acceptance are the medicines most needed; at other times, something active and fiercer. Neither are "true" or "better" or "more spiritual," but each an expression of skillful means we can call forth in response to the various challenges in our lives. The most effective, wise, and compassionate approach is oriented in flexibility, in which we can go in either direction in any particular moment, fully commit to experimenting with it for a time and remain open to switching to the other for further investigation.

The bottom line is we are never going to resolve the ongoing dialectic between acceptance and change, but that is okay, for resolution is not required but only our creative and conscious participation in the mystery as it appears. We can engage in both pathways and mine the wisdom found in each without the pressure of some idea that we're supposed to choose only one, that there is a "right" or "more spiritual" one, and that we must abandon the other. As alchemists of our own lives, we remain committed to the *experiment itself* and to feeling all the feelings that come as natural consequences to whatever action we take. If we lean too much in the direction of being, we will be asked to meet and tend to certain feelings and experiences; if we organize our lives in a way that privileges only becoming, we have another set of feelings and experiences to work with and integrate. As always, the invitation is not into certainty, resolution, or even simplicity but into the core of the contradictions, paradoxes, and complexities of the human soul.

AN EXPERIMENT IN CREATIVE SELF-EXPLORATION

If in a moment I am feeling incredibly sad and caught in despair about my life, I could practice dropping this story line and coming back into the present moment. I could feel my feet on the ground, become aware of my breathing, shift my awareness out of the narrative of "me and my sad life" and into the immediacy of the body, cutting into the trance that something is wrong in *this* moment. Yes, it is true that a feeling of sadness has come, but this sadness is not who I am. It is only a wave in the ocean of the fullness of being—temporary, transparent, and workable. I do not *equal* sadness, but I am aware in this moment that sadness is present. "I" am not sad, but I am aware that the sensation of sadness has come, as a visitor of my psyche and nervous system, complete with its own core beliefs, emotional moods, and behavioral impulses. But "I" am that open field of energy in which this and all thoughts and feelings come and go.

From the perspective of acceptance and being, we (temporarily) see through and let go of the colorful and seductive narrative about why we're sad or who did what to us or what it all means or how horrible our lives are—and come back here, now. We might even begin to discover how feeding this habituated, conditioned story line is aggressive toward ourselves, a defense against the underlying feelings that just want a moment of our presence and loving awareness. We come back to the sounds in the room, the tingling of the hands and feet, the breath rising and falling in the belly, and the vast space in which the entire display arises, dances for a short moment, and then dissolves. We meet this temporary wave of experience with present-centered, mindful, accepting awareness. We're not fueling the story line about what happened, why it happened, how could they do that, no one will ever understand me, but infusing our experience with a compassionate presence. With the intention to care for ourselves deeply, we renew our vow to not abandon ourselves in those moments when we need ourselves more than ever.

This is a perfectly valid experiment, an activity of wisdom and skillful means, and can yield tremendous perspective, clear seeing, and relief. It can open us into a freedom always, already here no matter what particular thought or feeling happens to be passing through.

We do not need to get rid of, transform, or "heal" our immediate experience but only to tend to it with mindful and kind attention. Doing so opens us to the possibility of seeing that our suffering and struggle arise not from the mere wave-like appearance of sadness but in our relationship with it. In other words, there is no suffering *inherent* in the temporary movement of sadness; rather, the anguish comes from *resistance* to what is here, from rejection of it, and from the long-standing emotional conclusions about what a wave of sadness means about us and our lives. Training in the art of compassionate presence is a real gift we can give to ourselves.

Alternatively, perhaps we don't get far with it, it doesn't really lead anywhere, the time is not right, we just can't do it, we're too activated, or we are drawn for some other reason to engage in a different way. After sitting, staying with, or meeting the sadness in a nonjudgmental, accepting state of presence, we are still struggling, we are called to an alternative exploration—not in rejection of the first experiment but as a partner to it. Somehow, resting in the nonconceptual awareness of the space in which the feeling emerges does not appear to be the most fruitful or skillful remedy in the moment, and we notice a longing to get closer, more involved, more intimate with what is happening. We sense there is something else calling to us, some other way to engage, navigate, explore, and learn from the uninvited visitor—some way in which returning to the present alone is not allowing us to befriend, attend, and open to the material to encounter it in its depth.

From this latter perspective, we make a journey *into* and *with* the sadness, separate from it (remember the alchemical *separatio*), and enter relationship with the intention to explore its textures, qualities, fragrances, and essences. As I mentioned earlier, for some, turning the emotion into a figure (young child, wise old woman, apparition of light, grieving man, etc.) allows for a more embodied and heartfelt exploration because it is not always easy to enter relationship with an abstract emotion.[3] Whether we personify the emotion, impulse, or image, we can use our conscious attention and awareness to unpack and unfold the content, becoming curious about it, dialoguing with it, listening, and asking questions: Why have you come, what do you want from me, what is your purpose, why are you emerging in this moment, what is your historical origin, what do you need to heal and transform, what have you come to show me about how I might be living my life and what I might have forgotten? To where are you pointing me? What message have you come to offer? Why do you keep coming back?

Through engaging directly, compassionately, and curiously with the *content itself*—not merely the background *context* in which it arises—we are able to practice a certain intimacy with the visitor as it moves within the layers of experience, discovering how and where it resides in our bodies, what core beliefs it holds about us and our relationships, what images and moods it is tied to, and what impulses or behaviors it "asks" us to engage with in response to its appearance in our lives. We're not just disidentifying from or "staying with" the urge or feeling as a transitory, impermanent, vivid display of awareness and returning to the present moment, but we're being called into something more dynamic. We become curious about the sadness, for example, or the rage or shame, and want to *know it*, explore it from lots of different angles, listen to it, touch it, be touched by it, and allow it to unfold and share its essence, messages, guidance, secrets, fears, longings, and information. In this pursuit, we discover it is not some enemy come to harm us, some error or mistake we must dispose of or convert into joy but a part of us that longs to return home. It carries its own integrity and value and is a potential source of meaning and new vision.

Most importantly, we do not have to take sides. Instead, we allow ourselves to meet our experience with newfound levels of openness and interest, encouraged by a love of the truth and approaching our sacred human experience by honoring multiple perspectives. We let go of the fantasy that with the right understanding, insight, or realization we will resolve the great archetypal opposites of being and becoming, or that we need to limit the ways in which we tend to the soul, especially in its more challenging or confusing expressions. The goal here with our inner work is to generate movement in the psyche, in the soul, to unfreeze what might have become frozen, unlock something that might have become locked, and liberate something that might have become stagnant. Both mindfulness-based meditative inquiry and imaginal, psychological approaches are capable of facilitating movement when we have become stuck and open the doors of perception so that we might see, feel, and sense in a new way. Through a variety of doorways, we make discoveries inside and around the challenging experience, at times attuning to the context or ground in which it arises and at other times allowing its qualities and fragrances to unfold in great detail as it reveals its innermost essences to us.

THE VAST TERRITORY OF THE HEART

Let's explore this landscape a bit more together as it requires some repetition, engaging a variety of different images, metaphors, and language for us to begin to have a felt sense of the territory. It takes practice to rewrite old, out-of-date pathways, adjust the lenses of perception, and become artists of a new reality. At times, with mindful awareness, we observe the visitors and energies of the inner world as they emerge, color the landscape for a short while, and then dissolve, tending to this organic movement with compassion, acceptance, and kindness. We allow ourselves to just be, for *this* moment, to call off the search, and to let go of the exhaustion of a life oriented in unending becoming. We attune to the unfolding, embodied flow of thought, feeling, and sensation exactly as it is, without any agenda to manipulate, interpret, change, or even "heal" it, shifting awareness out of the stream of content itself and back into the field of open, spacious awareness in which all form comes and goes. We step off the battlefield for a few minutes or seconds and realize the great liberation in this, in the natural perfection of one complete moment.

At other times, the invitation is into the very core of the content itself, into its color and texture, into the uncertainty and aliveness of the relational world, more oriented in exploration than rest. It is a bit messier here, yes, but the call is into a different level of intimacy. Here we are less concerned with the background field or the context in which the material arises but with *the content itself*: how it emerges, takes expression in the world of time and space, and unfolds meaning, messages, guidance, and symbols relevant to our lives. We dive head- and heart-first into the content with curiosity and passion, drawn not to "just be" aware of it but to meet the visitor in a more energetic and even emotional way, interested and curious to become more and more intimate with it, to use our creative and imaginative faculties to mine the depths. We can use the mind as a vehicle of relationship, to think creatively and in new ways, to discover meaning and take new perspectives, and to more actively reorganize the characters, plots, story lines, and narratives; to play with the content and dance it into new form. There is such richness and aliveness in this.

Sometimes yin, sometimes yang. Sometimes being, sometimes becoming. Sometimes accepting, sometimes transforming. But never is the mystery resolved or do we come up with some ultimate answer because we don't need to take sides or choose in a way that results in fragmentation or rejection of its opposite. Both primordial energies are a part of the human person, each holy and sacred in their own way, each valid and worthy of our interest and care. Yes, the journey will feel contradictory at times as we navigate this unknown middle ground, but that is not evidence of error or mistake but only of how vast the territory truly is, of how majestic the human heart really is.

Each of these orientations is valid and is a potential source of useful information for our unique journey. We need not abandon one for the other but engage both with curiosity and presence, as experiments in self-awareness. At times we will give everything we have to one side, only to let it go and fully embrace the other in a later moment. It is perfectly natural to want to improve our sense of self, relationships, emotional experience, work lives, financial situation, physical health, relationships, and so forth. We can honor this human desire and work diligently to achieve these things, while simultaneously exploring the reality that our lives are more than endless self-improvement projects. There is something here *now*, already whole and complete, shining out of the chaos and the mess of our lives exactly as they are. We can honor that even if none of these things was able to truly change, we still have a human heart and mind and what we need at the most basic level to feel alive and live in a way that embodies great meaning, dignity, and sacredness. We can accept that we want to change *and*, at the same time, fully engage with our lives even if that change for whatever reason proves not possible, and we do not fall into the conclusion that we've done something wrong or have failed if we can't manifest all the changes we want. In the end, we might or might not be able to shift, transform, or even "heal" in all the ways we long for and desire, but even in this somehow we are able to know and live from that part of us that is changeless, not in need of transformation, and already healed. And we just bow to the mystery of that.

STORY, DREAM, AND AWARENESS

I've been speaking about these two primary ways of working with our experience. The first is rooted in meditative awareness, in which we're not oriented in exploring our interpretations or reflections *about* our experience but rather tending to its nature by way of direct perception. We are more curious about the *context* in which our thoughts, feelings, and sensations arise and dissolve and less with their specific *content*. Here, we're training ourselves to return over and over into immediacy, openness, acceptance, and noninterpretive apprehension of raw, naked experience as it arises moment to moment.

The other way is a bit messier and more alchemical—more complex, darker, and nuanced, oriented in the depths of soul rather than the heights of spirit. It recognizes that we human beings are storytellers by nature and invites us to honor and illuminate the ways we are dreaming our lives, how we're imagining things, how our entire psychic life is being organized under the surface. Here, we *are* interested in the content, its specific, particularized, concrete forms, qualities, signatures, and fragrances, not merely the context in which it arises. From this latter perspective, the invitation is to travel all the way into the core and the centerless center, opening with curiosity into the ways we have come to imagine reality, the mythical figures with whom we are traveling, and the archetypal images that underlie our experience. It requires a real care and love of the story itself, of the dream and the drama (yes, even the drama!), the imaginal characters and plots and subplots, the crescendos and resolutions.

Remember, this latter inquiry does not mean that we become fused or enmeshed in the content or identify with it as who we are in some absolute sense, but by way of the alchemical *separatio* we differentiate from it so that we can get to know it intimately while not drowning in or becoming flooded by it. This potential fusion/identification is one of the concerns of the meditative traditions regarding working directly with the content in the ways described here, which is reasonable and warranted. It can actually take quite a bit of practice, concentration, and awareness to engage in imaginal work without fusing with the images, which training in mindfulness and meditation can support.

Mindful decentering, defusing, and returning into the body, dropping the story line and returning to the present moment, to the physical sensations, and the breath can be powerful medicine to cut through habitual thinking and conditioned patterns of suffering. A lot has been written about the power of meditation, both in the scientific and popular literature, and I encourage nearly everyone I work with to learn and practice mindfulness, given its effectiveness in regulating attention as well as helping cultivate acceptance and self-compassion. And in its highest potential, mindfulness helps to cut through unnecessary suffering and reveal a freedom always, already here as the birthright of all beings.

From another perspective, some are called by way of curiosity, fascination, and a real interest in the *content* of the dream, not just the discovery that we are in fact dreaming. From this side of things, we're not focusing on how quickly we can "wake up" from the dream (an interesting and valid journey, to be sure), but deeply curious about the images and figures and about the precise landscapes that psyche has sent to us by way of the dream. You can ask questions such as: What is the soul trying to say to me? How have I come to imagine myself and my life, others, and the world? What is the mythic or archetypal ground from which I am living my life? How are these images and figures, as they appear in fantasy and dream, inviting me to enlarge my life, live more creatively, beautifully, and in a way that honors what my soul truly wants? The metaphor here is one of illumination, to bring light, perspective, warmth, and space to the stories, images, and beliefs that shape the way we navigate the world. For from this illumination and compassionate, clear seeing we can then make a conscious choice to update the narrative, discover a new myth or tale to live by—more inspiring, creative, and alive. We can dream a new dream and weave a more cohesive, integrated, real-time, kind, magical, imaginative story. In this way, we do not merely rest as the witness of our experience (which can be quite healing in its own right) but become artists of a new world. We become a poetic, engaged, caring witness and a fully embodied, messy, and glorious participant simultaneously.

Part of the challenge and potential shadow side of practices and orientations organized exclusively around returning to the background field or context of awareness is that we can lose touch with the rich-ness of the inner world, the wisdom and creativity in storytelling, in the figures of the dream, and in the sparkle of the imagination. And as a result, we can lose touch with the richness and unique landscape of our own subjectivity and radical uniqueness. Yes, we might find some peace, clarity, and acceptance, so very important and healing, but in my experience bringing together these approaches provides the most effective and powerful foundation for a life of depth, creativity, and meaning and allows us to connect with others and to help them in ways we might not be able to imagine ahead of time.

One of the concerns about working with the narrative (i.e., the way we've come to articulate and make sense of our experience) and the lenses through which we have come to perceive ourselves, others, and the world is that it can become overly mental or theoretical and pull us out of our immediate, embodied experience. The worry is that we spend so much time interpreting and understanding our experience that we lose touch with the magic of just one present moment, with the aliveness of the senses and more intuitive knowing. This is a valid concern. For me, the work with narrative is embodied, imaginal work rather than merely cognitive or thought based. This is not to say that the mind does not join us on our inquiry; it very much does and *must*. Being able to use the mind to vision and think clearly and creatively is essential. There is a strong antimind tendency in contemporary spirituality worthy of deconstructing, or at least examining, in a more nuanced way. In large part, through imagination and creativity, a new poem is received, a new story is able to tumble out of the stars and into, through, and as our lives.

The spiritual journey by its very nature is radically unique and will never assume a one-sized-fits-all approach. The territory of psyche and the heart is just too vast to conform to any prefabricated practices or beliefs and must be explored by way of primary, first-person experience. The contemporary landscape is filled with all sorts of ideas and concepts about what it means to be a "spiritual" person, and we must find the courage to question even the most sacred of these ideas, trusting the path of direct revelation as we come to have more and more confidence in our own unique experience. There are an infinite number of ways to open to, touch, and enter the mystery, and the right way for us might look quite different than that of our friends, family, or even our spiritual teachers. It can take an incredible amount of experimentation, over a lifetime, for the path to unfold and reveal its fruit.

In the final few sections of this chapter, I want to invite you into a shift in perspective, into a vast field in which you might open your senses, listen, feel, and attune with the aliveness of this sacred now moment. Here, you need not make any effort to understand or enhance your present experience; you can take a break from the seemingly unending journey of self-improvement in all its forms. Here, you are invited to step into a whole different container or vessel altogether, one that is emergent, dancing, playing, and expressing itself and its qualities in the shimmering here and now. The remainder of the chapter is an invitation in Being itself, oriented not in improvement or even understanding but in the mystery and beauty of the unfolding now.

At some point on our journey, we might hear a call to set aside the beliefs, teachings, and practices we've gathered throughout our lives, for just a moment, and rest. The call asks that we hit the reset button and take stock of where we've been, where we are, and where we're headed. This "rest" is not passive, cold, or resigned but lit up from within, fiery, engaged, and caring. Without making the activity of seeking wrong or making some grand heroic decision to "stop searching," we open to a more paradoxical invitation that comes roaring out of the thundering silence. For just a moment, some trance is broken, a spell that has had us leaning into the next moment is undone, and we come face-to-face with what is *always, already* here.

Just what this is must be discovered by each of us in the fire of our own direct experience, and we cannot take anyone's word for it. It is a rest and an aliveness that is not the product of a future movement in time, further understanding or realization, or improvement of ourselves or our circumstances in any way. In this moment, we're taken inside a dimension of experience in which we remember to participate in the miracle of being able to see, to hear, to feel, to breathe, and to know that we are alive. Here, we connect intimately with that part of our selves that was never *unhealed, untransformed, or unfree*—not in a way that is dissociative, dismissive, or in denial of the real struggles we face but in honor of the *entirety* of what we are, recognizing in some mysterious way this moment already contains everything we could ever want or need. It is a moment out of time, really, and might last for less than a second, but we are drawn to bring more awareness and more care to this dimension of experience, at times even feeling a longing or ache that pulls us into itself. Something mysterious, magical, alive, and sacred is wired into this moment by its very nature and carries the fragrance of the holy.

Feel your feet on the ground, open yourself to the sky above and the earth below, listen to the sounds as they arrive as visitors from some other place, touching you and opening you to the fullness of now. No need to take on some new belief or metaphysical orientation. Just slow down and open to the completeness of this moment. There is something precious here that is not the product of further searching or improvement. This moment need not be fixed, cured, or healed but attuned to with senses wide open.

In these now moments, in which the search is temporarily surrendered, something else is granted permission and space to emerge, some causeless miracle already wired into this moment exactly as it is. If we observe carefully with cleansed perception, we might discover that it is not *us* surrendering, as if that were a choice we were making or an action that we could take, but that somehow we are participating in a great surrender always, *already* occurring. We are not surrendering as an act of will but *being surrendered* by something vast. Although we cannot "do" the surrendering, we can prepare ourselves to participate when it appears.

We are like the alchemist no longer able to tell: Am I inside the vessel looking out? Or outside looking in? Or am I the material itself, being shaped and woven and crafted by the Beloved One, helping him or her or it or they to provide a spark of light or a particle of love to actually make it here into the world of time and space, to help this place in even some small way?

We each have a unique way to help another, through taking the risk to give our art to this world. Whether we "believe" in it or not, or whether we feel broken or whole, within the very center of the broken shards of the heart the illumination awaits. This turning Home, this risk, this work of releasing spirit from matter that the alchemists, poets, and mystics model is never done for ourselves alone but for life everywhere. For suffering everywhere. For the ancestors and those carrying lineages of intergenerational trauma. For the ones we see here with our physical eyes. For the ones not yet come, waiting for conditions to ripen. And for the earth herself, the waters, forests, moon, sun, and stars.

It's important to remember, as I stated earlier, that for me these references to "spirit" and "matter" and their relationship are all metaphors and images we can work with, inside, and around rather than metaphysical ideas to believe in or takes sides with. For the alchemist, there is a fantasy that spirit is found within matter; the alchemical invitation was to realize the ultimate nonseparation of spirit and matter, to "redeem" the spirit within nature, to see the spirit alive there. In this realm of imaginal experience, we "materialize spirit," ensoul and embody it, while we simultaneously "spiritualize matter." But again, the main point here is that these are metaphors, images, and fantasies we are invited to play with as we sense which doorways are most resonant for us. As always, we're invited not to take these ideas and this language literally, necessarily, but as portals into a deeper, richer, and more nuanced exploration of the dimensions of soul.

At times, we will need to exert effort to remember, to cut into a busy day of external doing and ruminative, repetitive thinking in response to becoming hooked into emotional reactivity or caught in the seemingly endless to-do lists of the inner and outer worlds. We *remember to remember*, pause and breathe deeply, open our senses, and reenter that state of pure wonderment. Yes, you might even have to schedule it! Perhaps set an alarm (a mindful-sounding bell, of course) on your mobile device or computer to remind you of a possible miracle unfolding nearby. A background hum is always sounding and dancing just beyond the spin and madness of the world, revealed in one moment of pause and pure listening. This listening, however, takes place not only with our ears but with our entire bodies, our breath, and our hearts. Only you can discover what this extraordinary listening looks and feels and smells and tastes and sounds like for you.

BEYOND SELF-IMPROVEMENT

This deep, embodied listening and attunement reveals an ancient invitation to take a break from *doing*; from trying to become a better person or desperately improve our lives; from needing to understand, accept, transform, or heal, for just *this* moment. It doesn't mean permanently ending the search for a transformed life, for a better world, or for healing and awakening. But just for now, see what it is like to stop *trying* to be at peace, to figure out what is wrong with you, and open to the completeness of this moment as it is, even if "what is" is intense, disturbing, uncertain, and unknown. Stop thinking *about* your life and begin *living* it, for just this one moment.

The intimacy, connection, and meaning we long for is found in *living*, not in orbiting around the life erupting out of the center. This is not to say there is no place for thinking about our experience; there very much is. The invitation is to allow ourselves to experiment with multiple modes and ways of being—at times interpreting, analyzing, and evaluating and at other times *resting in being itself*. To really see and feel this difference in an embodied, experiential way can bring great insight, creativity, and aliveness into our experience.

For just one moment, allow the quest for understanding and improvement to shift into the background and provide sanctuary for the emerging experience of now. You can return to transforming and healing in a future moment; it will all be waiting for you.

Just as an experiment, open into this unknown landscape for a few hours, or for a day or a week, not in some reaction *against* improvement, as if it were "wrong" or "unspiritual," but as an archaeologist of soul, to experience yourself afresh and to listen, to sense, to feel what is wanting to be met in a new way, as participatory research into your own heart.

It can be a disorienting and alive place because it can feel so groundless when we are not organizing our experience around improvement of ourselves or of the moment. That has become such a familiar axis around which we spin. Paradoxically, it can reveal the earthiest ground, where we are already being held by something vast. It can feel like we have come home, but in the next moment we can feel completely lost.

When the urge to improve, resolve, transform, or heal becomes overwhelming, take a moment to marvel at how amazing the power of this habit is—with no shame, no blame, no judgment, no attacking your vulnerability. Just gently return to the ground and see that even becoming "lost" is a sacred experience we are given out of love in order that "found" can emerge, only for "lost" to return yet again. The cycle of lost and found is not some grand error or cosmic mistake, but the unfolding of the beloved in the world of time and space.

Love does not have some grand bias for "found" over "lost" but sends each as an expression of its essence to reveal to us one of its magnificent and unique qualities. The question, then, is not how to replace "lost" with "found" but to what degree we are willing and able to participate fully in "lost" as it appears, not to dismiss or reject it but to care deeply about its fragrances and contours, curious about its nature, its meaning in our lives, and what it has come to show us.

Slowly, over time, you might notice your center of gravity shifting, but just what it is shifting *into* remains a mystery, an emanation of the creative, quantum unknown. The invitation is to commit to forty-eight or seventy-two hours without engaging in *any* inner work or improvement practices. For this short period of time, no meditation, spiritual books (including this one), mantras, affirmations, attracting, or manifesting. No effort to accept yourself, to forgive anyone, or to become grateful. No visualizing, breathwork, tending to your chakras, or trying to understand or improve yourself or this moment in *any* way.

For some of us, this can be an incredibly disturbing (and fascinating) experiment. We might discover in an experiential way how much of our time and energy is oriented not in fully *participating* in life but in our attempts to *improve* the moment (or ourselves) in one way or another. If we are not improving, will we cease to exist? Who are we if we rest in this moment? If we do not "heal" or transform ourselves or the moment, what do we find? The invitation is not to "answer" or resolve these questions but to break open to their mystery and depth as we step into the unknown, where new vision is found.

It can be disorienting to remove the reference point of organizing our lives around improvement, transformation, and healing because we are left naked with ourselves. Even sitting in a room for thirty minutes and doing absolutely nothing, we can be tempted to start subtly doing yoga or qigong, breathing in a certain way, chanting softly, entering a meditative state, practicing gratitude, discovering laws and secrets, calling in our soulmates, and manifesting abundance. We might even begin to notice how "just being in the present moment" can carry with it a subtle agenda. Just who and what are we if we allow ourselves to step outside all of this, not permanently, but for just a short time?

THE SPACE AROUND OUR EXPERIENCE

Especially for those of us committed to transformation and healing, it can be quite a discovery to see how much of our life energy is put into the creation and maintenance of a *process* relationship with life, as opposed to actually *living* it, how much we are used to doing, interpreting, getting somewhere, and resolving something. Attending to our inner projects. Fixing ourselves. Remedying some fundamental flaw in what we are. Mastering things, empowering ourselves, completing inner to-do lists. Attracting things, replacing other things, shaming ourselves for not doing it right, and *operating* on the present moment.

I want to make it clear I am not asserting that there is anything wrong with our seeking, our desire for improvement, for healing, and for spiritual awakening. Not at all. In fact, I see it as perfectly natural, wired into us, and a sacred aspect of our human nature. No shame, no blame, no self-attack. The invitation is just to see with more subtlety what we're doing, what's motivating us, and the unconscious beliefs underneath it all and to love ourselves enough to slow down, even to stop for a few days or weeks so that we might see what is happening with new perception. Just a simple experiment. Nothing more. Nothing new to believe in; you're not being asked to give up your practices forever. With curiosity and compassion as your guide, just see.

As we experiment in this way, *at times* we might notice ourselves becoming more curious about the *space* in and around our thoughts and emotions rather than their specific details and particularities. It's as if our center of gravity shifts from the *content* to the *context* of our experience, or to *awareness itself*. What a strange experience. On the one hand, totally fresh, spontaneous, and unfamiliar. Less heavy, more open, and expansive. Alive. Not so weighed down by the burdens of the past or the worries of the future. On the other hand, we might recognize this way of being. Perhaps there is an ancient memory of this deep level of rest and nourishment from another place or time. In ways that language cannot really touch, somehow awareness becomes foreground and content becomes background. The bottom drops out from underneath us as well as out of the top and sides. We've arrived home, but it is not the home we *thought*. It is a home crafted of space, not one oriented in improving but in just being here and in recognition of the majesty of that.

A VAST MEADOW

In this landscape of now, we might notice our orientation shifting out of a journey from "here" to "there" to resting in a more natural state strangely already complete, compassionately tending to reality as it is, rooted in curiosity and the love of pure being. Thoughts continue to come and go—as do feelings, emotions, sounds, images, memories, and sensations in the body. But they are coming and going in a vast meadow of space—not in a cold, distant, void-like space but one filled with the qualities of presence and warmth. This space is fertile and pregnant, emanating possibility and a quantum sort of potentiality. In some inexplicable way, we sense that we are *already* healed, *already* fully awake in the immediacy of this moment, and even if we wanted to, we would have absolutely no idea how to improve this moment or what that would even mean.

In a way that can seem paradoxical to one seeking further understanding, clarification, and transformation, the "healing" and "awakening" have nothing to do with the presence or absence of *any* particular experience. The grand replacement project, in which one thought or feeling is interchanged with another, is no longer the axis around which we orient. Rather, whatever internal experience appears is met with curiosity and by way of relationship—even if difficult, challenging, and intense, it is experientially known to be workable, valid, and an expression of creativity and intelligence. But how could this be? What happened to the compelling and persuasive conviction that something is wrong? Surely, there is something still wrong. Isn't there? I know I can find it—just give me a minute, and I'll remember what is wrong with me, what needs fixing, curing, healing, transforming, and shifting. This can be an interesting place in which to find ourselves, unsure of whether there is something wrong with us, uncertain whether something needs to be transformed or healed or whether these images, lenses, and metaphors are no longer the ones we are engaging with in our interaction with self, others, and world. It's not so much that we've made some decision about them by way of reaction or willful dismissal, but that somehow they're no longer occupying the foreground in the way they used to.

In these moments, we become aware of a primordial sort of trust in life and in our own experience. Nothing need be cultivated, generated, healed, or transformed *for right now.* It does appear that some sort of shift happened, but it did not arise from our own will and effort. It did not follow in some causal way from something we *did* or even from our intention. We did not shift something; it feels more like something *shifted us,* or the background context in which we find ourselves shifted and took us along with it. But even the idea of a "shift" crumbles away into the vastness of the moment.

To stay with this much openness requires new levels of curiosity, courage, and perhaps most of all a radical friendliness toward ourselves and our immediate experience. It can take some time to get used to, fully trust, and allow the decades-old organization around improvement to be washed away in the great ocean of what we are. Without this new lens and profound self-compassion, we're not going to be able to open into the unknown and stay with the groundlessness of having no reference point other than awareness itself. We are so used to having some stable center point around which to orient and look back to confirm who we are.

When the ways we come to imagine ourselves, others, and the world fall away in a moment of spaciousness and illumination, we find ourselves in a liminal space, in between worlds, not sure where to seek refuge and orientation. Without these familiar positions, we are in new territory. Although this environment can feel alive and even exciting, it can also be disorienting and even a bit terrifying when the rug of the conceptual is pulled away, especially if it is not replaced by another rug on which we can find solidity. In one way, there is no ground to rest on, yet in another, the ground is everywhere. But because it is not separate from what we already are, we do not always easily perceive it, not to mention live, love, and work from such an open, undefended place. It is like asking a fish if she knows about this thing called water. "Oh, yes, I've heard of it," she replies. "I will be on the lookout."

In the next chapter, we'll continue to unpack the subtleties of our beliefs and practices as we build the foundation for a spirituality of our own—authentic, creative, unique, and alive for each of us, connecting us with the heavens while grounding us in the earth. Although we can and will always draw on the experience of the great yogis, meditators, soul explorers, and mapmakers of the inner world, the invitation is toward discovering our own unprecedented journey, oriented in the depths and the fire of our own immediate experience.

7

TOWARD AN EMBODIED, EMOTIONALLY SENSITIVE SPIRITUALITY

OVER THE PAST FEW DECADES, researchers have explored a phenomenon in which engagement with spirituality is seen (in part) to serve a defensive function in the avoidance of emotional vulnerability, relational trauma, and psychological wounding. Coined in 1984 by psychologist and Vajrayana Buddhist practitioner John Welwood, the term "spiritual bypassing" refers to the use of spiritual beliefs and practices to circumvent a direct, conscious relationship with painful feelings, unresolved psychological wounding, and unmet developmental needs.[1] With many millions each year taking up practices such as yoga, mindfulness, meditation, shamanic journeying, and other forms of self-development and spiritual growth, it is important to cultivate an awareness of the dynamics of this phenomenon and how as individuals and communities we can most skillfully respond to its varied manifestations. To pretend this isn't happening or to close our eyes to its expressions can have profound consequences, as many have discovered.

Although it was a radical discovery some decades ago that spiritual practice, even the most advanced and sophisticated forms of yoga and meditation, were often unable to penetrate the deepest layers of psychological, emotional, and somatic wounding, this notion has come to be more accepted in contemporary spiritual subculture. Over the years, many have discovered that spiritual practice alone is not able to fully or most skillfully address all forms of suffering. Because most of our developmental challenges originated within the context of interpersonal misattunement, many believe we must look to the relational field itself to get at the root of personal healing. Research has also suggested that "earned security," that transformational journey from insecure to secure attachment, occurs primarily by way of relationship, whether formally in the context of psychotherapy or in intimate, romantic partnership or even close friendship. The implication is that wounds and blockages that arose relationally are not necessarily resolved or best untangled through solo-based, contemplative practice alone.

Fundamentally speaking, spiritual bypass emerges when the spiritual line of development is emphasized at the expense of attention to other, critical areas. Consequently, through the mature inclusion of experiential work in somatic, cognitive, emotional, moral, and interpersonal domains of experience, spiritual bypassing can be starved at its source. Although the relative priority of developmental levels in a person's life will shift both temporally and situationally, the underlying notion remains: if we allow any of the developmental lines to overshadow others, pushing them into the background, ignoring, or "bypassing" them, we do so at our own peril. In turning away from any of the fundamental areas of human development, we create fertile soil in which spiritual bypassing can flower.

We must remember that more spiritual practice is not always the most wise, skillful, or effective remedy for working with developmental trauma and other types of relational wounding or the right medicine for all forms of suffering. In fact, certain types of inner work can overwhelm the body and nervous system and constellate retraumatization. More meditation, more resting in the present moment, more forgiving, and more accepting are not always the right prescription in a particular life at a particular time. This realization is not always easy to let in for those of us deeply committed to our spiritual lives, but in the end doing so can be a great act of both wisdom and compassion.

THE BRIGHTER THE LIGHT, THE LARGER THE SHADOW

It might come as no surprise that spiritual groups and communities can be a breeding ground for the manifestation of spiritual bypassing. This occurs, for example, when emotional and interpersonal development is usurped by an emphasis on cognitive and transpersonal experience, with the former relegated to a "lower" status as compared with "purer" and "more advanced" spiritual work. In many of these groups, methods of transformation and healing outside the ones sanctioned by the tradition are not encouraged—or are even frowned upon—leaving some members struggling to address issues such as low self-esteem, trauma, narcissistic injury, and the effects of insecure attachment. Those suffering in these ways are often critiqued for not having enough faith or commitment to the teachings and practices; however, the teachings and practices are only serving to further entrench them in organizations of experience not attended to with more faith and more discipline. Not to mention the chaos, abuse, pain, and unbridled narcissism we've all seen over the years with certain teachers and outright denial in their communities, including painful and devastating scandals in areas of money, power, and sexuality. The brighter the light, the larger the shadow, so they say.

Spiritual bypassing can almost always be observed in the ways in which we are avoiding or diminishing one (or more) developmental lines. In so doing, we attempt to go around these critical (and often messy) domains of human experience—such as the body, relationships, sexuality, emotions, parenting, money, and work—en route to the transpersonal and transcendent. An effective response (or preventative) to the phenomena of spiritual bypassing is an approach to our lives that addresses personal, interpersonal, *and* transpersonal dimensions of our human experience. In other words, we cannot leave out the personal (our developmental histories, historic core vulnerabilities, trauma, self-identity, and organizing narratives) or the relational (our capacities to allow another to matter, expectations in relationship, attachment wounding, organization around the experiences of abandonment and enmeshment) if we are interested in an embodied, fully human approach to spirituality.

Problems related to spiritual bypassing occur frequently in the lives of spiritual practitioners, usually in the form of dissociation or splitting off from unwanted feelings, bodily sensations, and habitual patterns of perception. As with all defensive behavior, we engage in spiritual bypassing to avoid pain, emotional vulnerability, and the anxiety underlying the deep sense of separation we feel from ourselves, others, and the world. All sentient beings appear to be wired, conditioned, and habituated to turn from that which is unpleasant and anxiety provoking. Although the stated goal of most spiritual systems is the reduction of suffering and the increase of freedom and peace, we can all make use of these teachings and practices to reject parts of ourselves and experiences too painful to confront directly. Because the dynamics and expressions of spiritual bypassing can be quite subtle—and often unconscious—its movement frequently goes undetected. Illuminating this territory, not with shame, blame, and increased self-aggression but with curiosity, awareness, and kindness is a great gift we can provide both ourselves and others.

DEFENSES AS ALLIES ON THE PATH

Whether we use the term "spiritual bypassing," it is most important to see into the ways our relationship with spirituality, personal development, and self-help teachings can be used to come closer to ourselves, others, and the world or to take us further way and support unconscious patterns of thought, feeling, and behavior. In some circles, the term has taken on a pathological tone, neither warranted nor helpful, in which we use the discovery of avoidance as yet another vehicle through which to practice self-aggression. In many ways, "spiritual bypassing" is no different than any other defense mechanism. It serves an important adaptive function and must be honored and respected as such, not attacked, shamed, and torn down in some glorious heroic enlightenment project. We can discover a tremendous amount of information in reflecting upon the ways we engage with certain teachings and practices to avoid pain, intimacy, emotional experience, and unwanted parts of ourselves. The goal is not to "get rid of" spiritual bypassing per se but to bring more consciousness (and compassion) to it so that its inevitable expressions can be used in service of mature spiritual depth.

If we're interested in this, we could take some time and ask: To what degree is my engagement with spirituality (or therapy or self-help teachings, etc.) bringing me closer to myself, to previously disowned feelings and shadow aspects of my personality, to the underlying core beliefs I have about myself, to my fears and longings around intimacy, and to the ways I have come to imagine myself, others, and the world? Alternatively, to what degree might my beliefs and practices be keeping me *away* from those parts of myself, promoting distraction and avoidance, and preventing deeper awareness of my own narcissism, blind spots, and unfelt feelings?

There are times when defending against difficult experience *is*, in fact, the most skillful way to respond to a situation in our lives. If, for example, we use certain meditative practices or journaling or breathing techniques to reduce symptoms of anxiety so that we can make it through the day, attend to our jobs, or be present with our children, is this "spiritual bypassing?" Are we "using" our practices to "get rid of" anxiety rather than work through and integrate it? Let us not answer too quickly. We must be willing to go deep into our own experience because the territory here is nuanced and subtle, for we can even use the concept of spiritual bypassing *itself* to attack parts of ourselves and reenact dynamics of self-aggression.

In psychodynamic practice, working with defensive organization takes an incredible amount of insight and the capacity to hold and navigate multiple and contradictory thoughts and feelings. The phrase "defense mechanism" has a fairly negative connotation in spiritual circles; however, we must remember the consistent invitation throughout this book that the goal is not to "get rid of" some unwanted aspect of our experience but to increase consciousness regarding what's going on. Training ourselves to see how we might be using our relationship with inner work to avoid certain aspects of our experience is intelligent and kind to ourselves and others. In this way, even our defensive organization, in this case in the form of spiritual bypassing, can be imagined as an ally on our path because it provides endless opportunities for deepening awareness.

Developmentally, spiritual bypassing is an effective strategy (as are all good defense mechanisms) through which we learn to care for ourselves, to honor the delicate nature of a traumatized nervous system, or to prevent too much feeling or anxiety to emerge too quickly, overwhelming us with buried experience we have not yet been able to integrate. The invitation is not to crash through the wall of our defenses but to approach them with widening perspective and love. This is not to say that they do not need to be brought into consciousness and transformed, but we can do so in an overall environment of curiosity and compassion rather than shame and self-attack.

EXPLORE . . . AND THEN REST

It can be helpful to differentiate psychological and spiritual dimensions of our inquiry as a way of orienting and ensuring that we are touching on as many aspects of our experience as possible. Whether we believe psychological work and spiritual practice are the same or different, it is clear they interpenetrate and affect each other. Some believe they are the expression of one seamless movement in the human person, and that might be true at a deep level. But it can also be useful to separate them to help us approach them in the most skillful way possible. By differentiating them in this way, we don't need to take any metaphysical position on whether they *are* or *are not* the same or different; it's really just an experiment that might help us to come closer to our experience and to understand the subtleties at deeper levels.

Psychological inquiry is oriented in our capacity to reflect on our experience—to step back and take a perspective on the core beliefs, organizing narratives, emotional and somatic experience, memories, dreams, and fantasies that shape the way we have come to see ourselves, others, and the world. Without this capacity for self-reflection, we become fused (or "identified") with our experience, embedded within it, and unable to enter spacious and creative relationship with the seemingly unending display of our thoughts, feelings, and sensations.

To return to our discussion in the previous chapter, psychological work (generally speaking) focuses upon the *content* of our experience and how it unfolds in our lives. It involves uncovering the ways we are making sense of our experience and the meaning we have prescribed to it. It might also involve understanding and reflecting upon the historical origins of the content and the unconscious lenses through which we engage important relationships, with the goal of making these lenses more conscious so that we can heal and transform out-of-date perceptions and narratives with more integrated and real-time ones that reflect our deepest insights and realizations.

Meditative-based inquiry, in contrast, is not as oriented in understanding and working with the *content* of our experience but attuning at deeper and deeper levels to the *context* in which it occurs. It is a pure, phenomenological inquiry in which we allow ourselves to apprehend whatever appears with warm, spacious, accepting awareness as it unfolds moment by moment in the here and now. We're not as interested in its implicit meaning or entering a dialectic relationship with it, investigating why it has come, its historical origins, what purpose it serves in our experience, and so forth. It is just an open, naked attending to our experience as it flows in through the doors of the senses. In meditative awareness, we aren't as interested in the *meaning* of our unfolding experience but in its essence, in its ground.

Training ourselves to access, regulate, and integrate challenging experience—making sense of it and exploring its underlying meaning—is the heart of psychological inquiry, especially as it relates to material previously dissociated, disowned, or only partially metabolized. To provide safe haven for those aspects of ourselves to come home into awareness is a profound act of self-compassion—not so that we can merely recognize, accept, and let them go, but so that we can get to know them and explore their contours, purpose, and meaning in our lives.

Entering into noninterpretive, open, direct apprehension of the *nature* or *context* of our experience as it unfolds in each here-and-now moment—without any agenda to understand, transform, or heal it—is the essence of meditative inquiry. From this perspective, difficult, disturbing, and confusing experience does not arise to be healed *but to be held*, to be permeated with and soaked in loving awareness. Whether it transforms is a secondary concern, but what remains primary is the agendaless engagement with what is.

Most forms of mindfulness-based meditation (at least classically speaking) are generally not concerned with understanding, unpacking, making sense of, or exploring the *meaning* of the content that comes into awareness but returning to the object of meditation so as to not get tangled up in the content itself, in the endless display of discursive thought that flows spontaneously in the mind stream. Training ourselves to disidentify with repetitive thinking and painful feeling states is an important and helpful skill; however, the shadow side of this is slipping into dissociation and subtle pathologizing of psychic experience, which carries its own wisdom and information apart from its actual nature. If we dismiss or repress emotion and feeling as part of our meditation practice, we are not able to mine this intelligence, and we place the material deeper into the shadow, thereby creating the conditions for projection and future suffering. Although most meditative techniques, of course, do not have this as a goal and are not avoidant by nature, as I mentioned earlier, we can use *any* practice to further dissociation. The invitation, therefore, is not to abandon any particular practice we find beneficial but to engage it with eyes wide open as to its possibly unintended consequences.

Psychological inquiry invites us into an embodied intimacy with our experience but not so close that we fall in and become flooded, enmeshed, and retraumatized. The invitation here is into relationship, not identification, and healthy intimacy, not fusion; to allow ourselves to care deeply about what we're experiencing, to be willing to get messy, to stay with states of not knowing, to enter into the body and the heart and take the risk to see what is there. To set aside our fantasies of invulnerability, mastery, and power and lay ourselves at the feet of the mystery. To see that life would never ask us to "master" it but to open to it, dance, and play as its humble kindred traveler. To tend not only to the *nature* of our experience but also to its content, details, fragrances, and unfolding meaning. To be willing to go into the experience all the way, not just with pure awareness but with the creative faculties of the imagination and the soul.

TENDING TO THE VOICES WITH SOUL

It's so instinctive and automatic to equate the voices in our head with expressions of objective reality. We hear these voices throughout the day, and they can become especially loud in times of activation, overwhelm, and stress. We so quickly assume that if we think it, it must be true, especially those thoughts that have appeared thousands (millions) of times. But as the great yogis, meditators, and wizards of cognitive science have discovered, identifying with thinking (in the research known as "cognitive fusion") tends to result in a enmeshed state in which we lose perspective, become overwhelmed, and lose touch with the larger field of awareness in which all thought comes and goes. We forget that just because a thought or voice appears does not mean it is true. Although this is a simple enough concept to understand intellectually, to let it in at the deepest levels is an act of revolution. To allow this realization in even for a second or two can bring great relief to a frazzled nervous system.

What are these voices, anyway? Or, more precisely, *whose* are they? Are they ours? Our parents'? Ancestors'? Teachers'? Politicians'? Authority figures'? Celebrities'? Television characters'? When we slow down and turn toward them with curiosity, who do we discover?

Although the voices can be varied and cover many topics, one of the more common themes they express is that something is wrong— with us, with our lives, with our immediate experience—which we must urgently correct. This particular voice is sometimes described as the "inner critic," an archetypal figure that has visited human beings throughout recorded history. Although the specific language might be different, the underlying message, especially in a moment of activation, is often something like:

"Something is wrong with me. Even though I can't quite pinpoint what it is, I just know it. When all is said and done, I know that if I fully show another who I am, I will be abandoned, attacked, rejected, and remain lonely and unseen."

The first step always is to recognize that a voice is speaking—and not to confuse this voice with objective reality, with some ultimate truth. The reality is that it is one voice among many, one that often has historical roots in environments of empathic failure on the part of our early caregivers. In this recognition, we can slow down and realize that without a new level of curiosity, awareness, and perception, we will become entangled in the forest of habitual, conditioned thinking. Just *this* time, we will choose differently.

In the slowness and spaciousness of warm, embodied presence, we might come to discover that these voices carry and transmit inter-generational trauma, the passing of insecure attachment narratives through the psychic and genetic pools. Through repetition and loop-ing, they attempt to reorganize and make sense of painful experience. These "inner persons" long for us to hear them, get on their side, and somehow liberate them from the trance of nonlove, from the spell of "something is wrong." They have not come to harm us per se but for redemption.

I hope it goes without saying, but I'm speaking about a situation in which there really isn't anything "wrong"—you're not actually in danger, being attacked, or otherwise needing to take immediate action to protect yourself. If that is the case, by all means, set aside all this "inner" work and take care of yourself through whatever external behavior you must. Here, though, I'm speaking about a more common situation in which, in a relationship or at work or in a moment of stress, you subtly (or not so subtly) notice yourself attacking your own vulnerability, bailing out of your body, falling into a spiral of shame and complaint, blaming and practicing aggression toward yourself in a moment of emotional activation.

In this latter situation, which we all experience at times, we are invited into experimentation. We can experiment with allowing these voices to be there and infusing them with spacious, warm, curi-ous attention. "Ah, you again. Hello. Tea?" Through meeting them in open awareness, they might dissolve into the background field from which they came. When we step off the battlefield and wash them with space, they lose their charge. It's not so much that we "let them go" by way of some active spiritual process, but we bear witness as they let go of us when they are no longer kept alive through enmeshment with and fueling of an internal war.

At other times, we might be called to engage them with a hotter, more active flame, not as oriented in nonjudgmental, mindful attention but in relationship. A different medicine is asking to be applied; an alternative alchemical operation might be more skillful in the moment. The voices are calling for a more direct, penetrating, inquisitive, confrontational way of navigating the material that is oriented in our own integrity. We separate from the voices and open a dialogue:

"I am listening but will not fuse with you. I will not allow myself to be flooded by your dysregulating energy. But I am here. Why have you come? What do you need? Why do you continue to return? What are you afraid of? What do you feel you must protect me from? Let me free you from the burden you are carrying."

We allow the voice to take form as an image or a figure with whom we can dialogue as we move the psyche along, unfreeze what had become frozen, and separate from what had become sticky and fused.

Either way, each are valid experiments and worthy of our attention, inviting space, breath, and compassion into the relational field. Entering into the middle realms between repression and fusion, denial and flooding, suppressing and acting out, we allow these ones temporary passage into the tavern of the psyche and body, to then continue their journey onward.

In an act of love, we tend to them as they arise, and in an equally holy act, we allow them safe passage into the other world.

THE UNIQUE NATURE OF SPIRITUAL DISCOVERY

It is important to remember that inner work is unique to the individual and might not always conform to collective norms. Before we know it, we can fall into the trap of a one-sized-fits-all mentality, in which we

come to believe there is one remedy to the complexity of human suffering and the entire majesty of the soul is reduced to one explanation
and a singular form of medicine. In my experience, there is a tendency
to oversimplify the journey of healing and awakening, which fits com-
fortably into our fast-food consumeristic culture as a defense against
the anxiety that arises in the face of just how complex, mysterious,
deep, and nuanced the psyche and heart truly are. Although it is fash-
ionable to see the spiritual journey as "simple"—"Just be in the now,
just love everything as it is, just return to the present moment; it's so
simple!"—this is not my experience or the experience of many of the
great wisdom traditions. The human heart has endless dimensions and
chambers. Although we can appreciate the desire not to overcompli-
cate things—or to turn the journey into yet another vehicle through
which to accumulate endless information—we must also remain
vigilant to the movement, especially in our contemporary world, to
oversimplify and reduce the majesty of the soul to a few generalized
catchphrases. It requires a lot of courage and patience to embrace the
complexities and depths of the path oriented in the slow, nonurgent
maturation of the human heart. There is no rush to the finish line and
no need to patch up the mystery, resolve the contradictions, or wrap it
all up in a weekend of enlightenment experiences and nonthreatening
spiritual slogans.

If a certain teaching or practice is not working for you, before you
conclude you do not have enough "faith," "discipline," or "commitment" or you are "stuck in a low vibration" and your "ego is in the
way," pause and consider whether this teacher or teaching is the right
one for you, at this unique time and place in your life. Perhaps you are
not "lost in your ego" but in touch with your heart, your body, and your
innate intuition. As always, you cannot take anyone's word for it, but
you must go inside and bring forward as much discernment as you are
able, shining light into the darkened places and receiving the guidance found only there. It takes courage to trust in your own experience,

especially when surrounded by voices attempting to convince you that you have lost your way, that ego has got you again, and that you have no idea what you "truly need" to progress along some preprescribed path. Whether these voices sound your mom's and dad's or your therapist's, guru's, teachers', and politicians', they must be brought into the fire and heated with your own direct experience.

Forcing a methodology, belief, or practice upon another because we think it is the "best" or "most spiritual" (and then subtly or not so subtly shaming them when they cannot "follow" it) when they do not possess the developmental capacity or individual resonance to engage that practice is tremendously unkind, needlessly aggressive, and even violent in certain situations. It is one thing to honor the other's higher capacities and to never forget the brilliance of their true nature, especially in the face of profound suffering but another altogether to impose our views upon people in a way that does not honor their native intelligence, relative functioning, and current situation.

May we truly be there for the others we counsel and push them a bit, if this is our agreement together, but always remain aware of the possibility of sending them spiraling outside their window of tolerance. Before we act in a way that causes others to mistrust their own experience, let us commit to slowing way down, metabolizing those feelings and beliefs within ourselves that most need attention, and opening to what will truly be most beneficial for others, then act from that place.

Of course, all this goes for ourselves as well, when we judge or shame ourselves for not living up to someone else's ideas about the way our journey should be unfolding. And then we begin to mistrust our own experience as we privilege another's, often an enactment of early relational configurations colored by empathic failure. Of course we want to learn from others and push ourselves beyond what we already think and know, but there is a fine line between doing so and attacking ourselves when we are unable to fit into others' visions. We must illuminate this line and navigate it with fresh vision, discernment, and kindness.

EGO AS A PARTNER ON THE JOURNEY

Proper understanding and skillful use of ego-consciousness is vital on the path, and we must clarify what we mean by this term to fully grasp its importance. As always, we must vision and revision these and all worn-out spiritual concepts so that we can play and dance loosely with them, in a flexible and nonfixated way, in order that they serve our exploration rather than generate additional struggle and confusion.

Ironically, especially with traditions that emphasize the realization of "no self" or ego transcendence, it is not too difficult to make use of such teachings in an unconscious way to sidestep important developmental deficiencies and longings. Without adequate discernment, it is easy to make use of even our most potent spiritual experiences to hide out from aspects of the personality that could really use some illumination and attention, if not for ourselves, then certainly for the benefit of those around us.

It is essential to remember that the word "ego" is a concept, an abstraction. It's not a *thing*. We're not going to go into our immediate, embodied experience and find an "ego." It is already one step removed, dissociated from the experiential world. The "ego" is an interpretation of some psychic activity or process, not a phenomenological discovery of reality. This doesn't mean that we can't use the term to point to some aspect of our experience or to communicate with others. However, it is critical that we slow down and begin with the truth that ego is not a *thing* but a once-removed, abstract, generalized concept.

Generally speaking, because of great confusion regarding this term and owing to its many varied (and contradictory) uses, I try not to use it all that often. But when I do, I tend to do so in two unique ways. First, in a more functional sense, we can speak about the importance of ego *strength* or ego *capacities*, especially those that seem to be required to engage with the deeper layers of psyche.

If we're lacking in basic ego functioning—for example in certain forms of narcissistic or borderline organization (yes, we *all* have the potential to dwell at times within these parts of the spectrum)—we need to build that structure before we can most skillfully engage in "deeper" work such as uncovering unconscious patterns, withdrawing projections, transforming internal working models, and the varieties of meditative discovery and experience.

From this perspective, ego is responsible for stabilization of our personality and identity through time, reality testing, executive functioning, and the capacity to take on perspectives and reflect upon our subjective experience. Without adequate ego development, life can get pretty gnarly, pretty quickly. If we aren't able to navigate consensual reality and remember who we are when we wake up in the morning, we will inevitably fall into various states of fragmentation and even fall apart wholesale.

But more experientially, for me ego refers to the way we've come to *imagine* ourselves and by extension how we've come to imagine others and the world. These imaginal lenses are usually formed and maintained outside conscious awareness and within an intersubjective or relational field at the intersection of self and other. When all is said and done, who do I believe myself to be? This imagination is full spectrum and has cognitive, emotional, behavioral, somatic, cultural-historical, and archetypal aspects.

Given all this, wise and skillful psychological (and spiritual) work, then, asks that we illuminate these imaginative lenses of perception, and from that clear seeing we can make a more conscious choice to imagine, dream, live, and breathe from a different set of images, fantasies, myths, and lenses, ideally more integrated, current, accurate, kind, poetic, and representative of our brilliance as open, sensitive, unique, eccentric human beings.

So the common idea in some spiritual circles to "get rid of," or worse yet, "kill" the ego really doesn't make any sense, at least from this perspective. The way I conceive of the term is not in line with the notion that "ego" is some wretched, homunculus-like being inside of me who is horribly unspiritual, ignorant, of a "low" vibration, and all the rest of it that I need to root out and banish into the underworld. In terms of this death, who or what would be the executor? And if we were to succeed in sending it underground, do we not think it will rise up in less-than-conscious ways in its natural attempt to return to the larger ecology of what we are?

Rather, the invitation is to allow the ego to take its proper place as one voice, one figure, one reality tunnel among many in the rich land-scape of psyche. A critically important one, but not the only one. To give it a seat at the table but allow it to be relativized so that it can find its proper place and make its unique contribution while not usurping full control. The goal, then, would be to facilitate engagement, dialogue, dance, and play between the ego and the other images, figures, and ori-enting worlds of perception that make up the landscape of the soul.

SELF AND NO SELF

Teachings on "no self" remain some of the most misunderstood and potentially confusing in contemporary spirituality, especially for those struggling with some form of narcissistic wounding, a fragile sense of identity, or developmental trauma of any kind (i.e., many of us). Even for those not struggling with overt trauma, neglect, violence, or abuse, the imbalanced and ungrounded denial of subjectivity and nar-rative implied in the misunderstanding of these teachings can lead to unnecessary suffering. The meaning and radical implications of these teachings—the experiential revelation of the flexible, relative, con-structed nature of the self—are bandied about in catchphrases outside the context of the depth and complexity in which they arose. As a result, they can often become unwitting tools for the reenactment of early environments of shame, unworthiness, and self-aggression.

It's important to remember that teachings on the relativity of self were historically provided within a meditative context, often during long retreat, within a community of practitioners who had dedicated their lives to spiritual realization. Additionally, they were given at a particular time along one's journey, after certain basic achievements and maturity were realized, ethical as well as meditative. In Buddhist tradition, for example, it wasn't until some basic grounding in the *Hinayana* (stabilization in working with one's mind) that the *Mahayana* teachings on *shunyata* (the nonsubstantiality of self and phenomena) were given. It is said in the *sutras* (the teachings of the historical Buddha Shakyamuni) that many in attendance on Vulture Peak Mountain when the Buddha first gave these teachings, passed out, lost consciousness, or even stopped breathing because of their earth-shattering implications. Whether we take this literally or imaginatively, the point is that historically, teachings on no self have been considered advanced, deserving serious consideration before their application.

To extract these refined discoveries from the environments and contexts in which they were given presents a host of risks, as we see play out in the contemporary spiritual world. To present them to those with little experience, or who might have a variety of contraindications, is not usually the most skillful or compassionate approach. As I've discussed, it is quite natural at times to make use of even the most subtle teachings to confirm egoic organization, all the while believing we're transcending it. Catchphrases such as, "It's all an illusion, drop your sense of separation and return to the present moment," "There's no 'you' there to have trauma," "Who is the one that would be traumatized?," and similar misattunements tend to encourage spiritual bypassing because they generate confusion, retraumatization, and additional kinds of suffering. It is one thing to learn the language of no self and nonduality; it is another to embody the subtleties of the experiential realization and allow the ramifications of that to filter down in the relative vehicles of the body, feelings, relationships, emotions, money, family, and sexuality. We've all seen the tragic consequences of half-baked proclamations of "total" enlightenment, "full" nondual realization, "permanent" awakening, and so on, in fallen gurus and leaders of spiritual communities who get tangled up in scandals of all kinds.

For those with histories of denying their own subjectivity—or having it abused, neglected, or dismissed by way of disorganized attachment, narcissistic injury, and empathic failure of all kinds—teachings on no self can feel all too familiar: "Oh, I get it, I really am nobody! I really don't exist after all. It's true that I'm not worthy of existing. Even the gurus have confirmed it. I knew it!" Rather than leading to increasing freedom, compassion, and flexibility, these teachings—if understood and practiced in immature and disembodied ways—unconsciously become another vehicle by which to replay templates of early wounding. In this way, the liberating implications go unrealized and are unable to filter into the lives of practitioners.

Shaming or making wrong our interest in the stories we tell about who we are and how we've come to make sense of our subjective experience—popular in some modern forms of "awakening," "enlightenment," and self-realization—have a way of creating and entrenching a profound shadow. Like any effective shadow, it usually remains hidden outside awareness because we have an unconscious investment in not seeing into the depths. For truly seeing the contents of the shadow has a way of bringing down the egoic house of cards as well as the constructed states of enlightenment that, although of course in part genuine and authentic, are often filled with holes not all that pleasant to confront. To step into this territory has a way of liquefying the enlightened ego and is profoundly humbling.

SELF, EGO, AND SPIRITUAL PRACTICE

To engage certain psychological, emotional, and meditative practices, a certain degree of ego strength is usually required; otherwise, the practice can be unconsciously used in service of a more dissocia-tive function. Remember, we can make use of *any* teaching as a tool of illumination *or* one of avoidance. If we do not have a relative degree of stability in our sense of self, some techniques can further fragmen-tation rather than facilitate greater wisdom, compassion, and clear seeing. With certain meditation practices—for example, in which we dissolve everything into open awareness, return to the Self, rest fully in the present moment, and no longer identify with the passing display of experience—we must carefully discern whether we are in actuality engaging in avoidance, dissociation, and repression. It is not always easy to tell the difference because both transformative *and* avoidant functions can be served simultaneously. This sort of discernment is not often taught either in psychological or spiritual circles but is critical and goes a long way in supporting an integral realization and an expres-sion in the world that *include* the body, emotions, sexuality, family, money, and relationships. Even if we achieve profound illumination, that awakened consciousness isn't going to do much good if it can only be expressed through a "broken relative vehicle."[2]

We cannot assume that one particular way of meditation or inquiry is going to be the most effective for everyone, though this is a posi-tion some practitioners take, whether consciously or otherwise. "Just do this one thing, this one way, and it will solve all your problems. It's all you need." Even if the teaching does not say this overtly, it often implies as much. But this view does not honor the uniqueness of the human person and can lead, as many have discovered, to further suf-fering and struggle.

It is important not to confuse healthy development of the self—including emotional and relational maturity as well as the capacity to articulate an integrated self-narrative—with "being lost in the ego" and the attendant shame and misunderstanding resulting from that confusion. This area of inquiry is fraught with lack of discernment and misunderstanding, especially in the context of those approaches unaware or even dismissive of the critical role of psychological, emotional, somatic, and shadow work on any integral path of spiritual realization. Complicated further by conflicting meanings of the terms "self" and "ego," the whole enterprise can get a bit tangled. In short, it is essential that we work simultaneously on the development and maturation of a securely functioning psychological self along with an exploration of those more transpersonal dimensions of human experience. In other words, we should not dismiss, pathologize, or shame the genuine wish to improve our sense of self, life circumstances, experiences in relationship, and so forth, while at the same time open ourselves to bands of the spectrum not oriented in self-improvement but in the realization of the nature of the self and reality.

Confusing the healthy development and maturation of self with "getting caught in the ego" can generate a tremendous amount of unnecessary pain because we become lost in disembodied spiritual jargon and half-baked ideas that imply that developmental needs, narrative, subjectivity, and the reality of relational trauma are "all in the mind," "only a function of the ego," and so forth. That conflation can also lead to the misattuned ideation that we must not be doing the practices right or advancing on our spiritual path if difficult emotions "still" arise.

Even popular and wise-sounding spiritual aphorisms such as "fear is the opposite of love" can set up a war inside us because they (even if unintentionally) pathologize human emotions and prevent us from mining the wisdom found within even our most challenging feeling states. From this perspective, even the natural wave-like appearance of "fear" is not an enemy with which we must do battle in some spiritual war against love but an aspect of psyche that has come with information, an ally in our journey into the depths, if we will only slow down and turn toward it. It is the rejection of fear and the abandonment of the fearful one within that can generate so much suffering and struggle, not just fear itself, an organic function of any human nervous system.

Upon investigation, we might discover no suffering inherent in a temporary wave of fear but only in the war we've waged with it and in the habitual conclusions we've come to about what it is, what it needs, and what it wants.

HONORING THE MOST SKILLFUL MEDICINE

It is important that we bring as much discernment as possible to the way we engage with teachings such as "no self" to ensure we are not reenacting early environments of empathic failure, narcissism, and trauma or furthering pathways of dissociation. And it's prudent to discover if these teachings are the best medicine for a particular person (including ourselves) struggling in a particular way at a certain time. It is unkind to foist the view of no self onto a person when it is contraindicated, when they do not have resonance with it, or when they do not have the developmental capacity to embody its radical implications.

Of course, let us also stay open to and honor the ways such teachings can be helpful and supportive in loosening our identification with suffering-laden organizations of limiting beliefs, painful emotions, and unhealthy behavior. It is important to remember that we might never know in some absolute way whether there "is" or "isn't" a self, which would require us to take some sort of metaphysical position. We can know for sure, though, that for most of us the most phenomenologically accurate description is that we have a *sense* of self. For most of us, there does *seem* to be a self, and this felt sense needs to be respected.

In working with meditators, yogis, and seekers over the years—and in my own inquiry, analysis, and supervision—I have seen the ways that "transcendent" teachings can be used to serve a liberating realization. These teachings, especially if practiced in an embodied, integrated context, can be an incredible force in reducing suffering and in revealing freedom always, already here. However, in other situations this is not the case, and certain teachings unintentionally further dissociation and unconscious defense against emotional and developmental wounding of all kinds, propping up old circuitry of unworthiness, shame, and self-hatred. This is something I have discovered not only in my work with others but more importantly in the pain of my own experience. As one form of spiritual bypassing, teachings on no self are particularly prone to serving a dissociative function. The larger the potential for transformative awareness, the larger the potential shadow.

My invitation is to flood our relationship with these teachings with as much nuance, sensitivity, compassion, and insight as we can so that we may tap into the ways they can truly support a mature, comprehensive realization while simultaneously realizing that they can also be a quick trapdoor into the unconscious shadow. I hope that we can each find unique ways to compassionately confront and assimilate the contents of the unconscious, for if we do not do so, we will inevitably continue to reenact the templates of early emotional and psychic wounding and create additional suffering for ourselves and others.

Although our engagement with spiritual ideas, beliefs, and practices has so much to offer in our lives—including profound support for meeting our experience with new levels of curiosity, awareness, spaciousness, and compassion—as always we must remain vigilant to the ways we can use our relationship with spirituality to keep us out of difficult states of experience such as confusion, contradiction, complexity, and pain of all kinds. Like any other emotionally significant activity in our lives, we can use our connection with spirituality to come closer to ourselves *or* defensively as a way to avoid ourselves, others, and our own trauma and pain—to shield us from a raw, direct, naked relationship with life. Inevitably, at times we will engage with spirituality from the foundation of the latter, which in many ways is so natural, so human. We need not shame, judge, or attack ourselves when we notice that we are doing this but rather use this discovery as a doorway into greater awareness, depth, and compassion, never forgetting how much an authentic journey of awakening asks of us.

Increasing awareness of the ways we engage spiritual beliefs, teachings, and practices to distance ourselves from pain and unwanted aspects of experience is essential if our goal is to befriend ourselves at the deepest levels, the ultimate invitation of this book. By doing so, we further the overall aspiration of opening to the radical possibility that even our most challenging experiences contain guidance and wisdom, and these experiences are, in fact, allies on the path of transformation and healing.

A MAP WRITTEN INSIDE YOU

It's important to remember that spirituality is not a one-size-fits-all endeavor, in which one method or technique is the right medicine for each of us, in all situations. A whole spectrum of valid human experience must be tended to through multiple perspectives. Forcing ourselves (or another) to adopt a certain practice (teaching, teacher) when there is no psychic resonance to that approach, or it is contraindicated within one's immediate experience, or it doesn't address one's unique location on the developmental spectrum might be seen as an act of aggression or, in some cases, even violence.

As just one example that comes up frequently in those populations where there is an intersection of interest in psychotherapy and spiritual practice, with certain forms of trauma, awareness-based meditation isn't always the right remedy. Where there has been profound early empathic failure (resulting in insecure or disorganized attachment and traumatic rupture), "resting in open awareness" can easily overwhelm and retraumatize a sensitive nervous system and psychic organization.

This is not to say there is something "wrong" with awareness-based practices but only to suggest they are not the most skillful or compassionate in *all* situations. A prescription of "more meditation" in some cases might not be kind or effective; however, unfortunately, this is often the advice those struggling receive from (well-intentioned) meditation teachers without experience in this area. As a therapist who has worked with many meditators over the years, I have met with more than a few suffering individuals who became further entrenched in embedded traumatic organization from trying to meditate more or harder or longer, not to mention the shame and sense of failure they felt when their meditation practice was not able to overcome their trauma. Just to be clear, I'm a huge proponent of meditation and mindfulness-based inquiry for *most* of those with whom I work and speak. Again, I am not asserting that these practices are not helpful, wise, and liberating—they are. I'm also not saying that these practices, especially if modified a bit, cannot be helpful to those struggling with trauma. They can. In recent years, a heartening effort has been made to adapt meditative practices for those who might find traditional approaches not sensitive enough to their particular situation. The invitation here isn't into some rigid advocacy of positions but into flexibility, perspective, kindness, and skillful means.

At times, structure- or resource-building is most needed—supportive work to repair a fragile sense of self, traumatized nervous system, or tragic disorganized attachment. At other times, uncovering or depth work illuminating and integrating shadow and unconscious process, along with reclaiming experiential responsibility for that which had to be disowned at an earlier time, is most needed.

Sometimes a transpersonal way of exploration could be most indicated, one not oriented in working through our biographical history per se, whether it be by way of psychic, subtle, causal, or nondual pathways.[3] We might tend to this territory of the spectrum by way of active imagination, dreamwork, breath or subtle energy practice, shamanic journeying, certain forms of visualization of imaginal figures, or a particular type of yoga or meditation. As always, the invitation is into discernment and nonhomogenization.

The point here is that if you do not resonate with a particular way of working, or if it is not helping you or even harming you, trust yourself and the wisdom and integrity of your own body and psyche. Honor your experience. Slow down and revision. It is fine to experiment, of course, but there is nothing wrong with you if a particular method is contraindicated at a certain time in your life. It doesn't mean you've "failed," don't have enough faith, are incredibly "unspiritual," or have succumbed to a "low vibration." It means you are alive and listening, sensing, and longing to care for yourself in a new way.

Spirituality is unique to each human heart, nervous system, and soul. There is a map written inside you in a language that only you can decipher. A preprogrammed, secondhand discovery will never do. You're just too majestic for that.

8

DANCING IN
THE SHADOWS

*Sanctuary for the Unwanted
to Return Home*

MANY PEOPLE THESE DAYS ARE FAMILIAR with the concept of "the shadow" and the importance of including "shadow work" in any comprehensive path of spirituality and healing. Especially when we experience scandal within a community (or ourselves) involving sex, money, narcissism, and power, it becomes obvious that less-than-illumined aspects of the personality are alive and well behind the scenes in all of us that can coexist with a certain amount of wisdom, compassion, and clear seeing. As long as there is a physical body, there will be a shadow lingering nearby. Although the increased awareness of shadow dynamics is a positive development, as with all psychological and spiritual concepts, we must approach the situation with fresh vision, depth, and nuance, willing even to explore *the shadow of the concept of shadow* and not take anything at face value.

Briefly, the shadow is that aspect of the personality we *all* have (yes, gurus and "masters," even you) that contains those parts of ourselves that we do not like, that do not fit in to the way we want to be seen, and that contradict the public persona we wish others to see. It refers to the subtle (or not so subtle) narcissism, selfishness, power-hungry, addictive, unkind, and violent parts of the psyche that we have repressed and will do anything to defend against bringing into consciousness.

For example, as spiritual people, many of us believe that we should not be angry and that the mere appearance of anger is some clear evidence that we have failed, done something wrong, or are not nearly as spiritual as we think. Perhaps any show of anger as a young child activated rage in Dad or caused Mom to be anxious and pull away from us, or we were shamed by our spiritual teacher or community for "getting angry." Whatever the reason, we've concluded there is something fundamentally wrong with the feeling of anger; it just doesn't fit into our image as an evolved person, and therefore we place it into the shadow, where we do not have to experience it directly. Of course, this does nothing to the underlying anger except to allow it to build energy in the unconscious, where eventually it *will* come out, usually in less-than-ideal ways in which we project it onto others and generate a lot of struggle, pain, and confusion.

Obviously, if our intention is to know ourselves at the deepest levels and to meet our most unwanted experience with curiosity and warmth, we must cultivate a relationship to the shadow, which we do primarily though illuminating and tending to its *manifestations*. From this perspective, the shadow isn't some reified entity within us that we must find and battle. We don't really see "it" but rather its reflections. In the example above, if we have placed our natural human experience of anger "into the shadow," we might feel quite a lot of anxiety when anger arises within us; we prepare to immobilize our defenses such that the anger will stay buried, or we move to locate it in another. "No way, I'm not angry. But *he* is so angry. *He's* so full of rage, isn't he? You can just feel it." The good news is that we can learn to work with this anxiety and uncover what might lie underneath it. We can follow it back and find that submerged feeling we've spent so much psychic energy avoiding over the years (or decades).

If we want to discover the wisdom and creativity buried within our most intense emotions, we must provide a home for the unwanted parts of ourselves to return where they can be tended to with greater awareness, perspective, space, and compassion. Some believe we have an ethical responsibility to work with the shadow; otherwise, we will be sure to project, locate, and even unload it onto others and the world, which will only increase unhealthy aggression, violence, and suffering for ourselves and others.

POSITIVE EXPERIENCE IN THE SHADOW

Usually when we speak about parts of ourselves we have disowned and placed into the shadow, we're referring to less desirable material such as jealousy, rage, selfishness, and shame. As mentioned earlier, the shadow is typically seen as the dark repository for all the so-called negative aspects of ourselves—that is, our unhealthy dependency, unacknowledged narcissism, unmet hopelessness, and unlived lives. But it is not only negative qualities and aspects of our self that we defend against, dissociate from, and send into the unconscious. In addition, many of us have lost the capacity to access, embody, and express more "positive" experiences such as contentment, pleasure, creativity, empathy, compassion, intimacy, and sexuality.

Although this is more difficult to wrap our minds around, some of us have disconnected from the simple experience of joy, a spontaneous sense of elation at being alive. I'll never forget the first time I realized we could split off from the experience of joy, which came about when I was working with a man suffering from depression. What we discovered during our time together was how unsafe it was for him to express joy, how the experience of simple delight became tangled in his nervous system with danger and the likelihood of imminent attack against him.

During our sessions, there were times when we would both become aware of this simple, childlike, causeless joy coming to the surface as he was speaking about some experience he had, and how inevitably at some point that would constellate anxiety in him: he would quickly change the subject, generate some sort of conflict or complaint between us, "leave" the room and go back into a prior conversation, or even just close his eyes and start to meditate.

After this happened a few times, we became curious about what was going on and were able to explore it together. He was able to trace back early experiences of how his father reacted to his joy and excitement, becoming aggressive and enraged, demanding that he "grow up" and stop acting like "a baby." He came to see how he had equated feeling full of life and natural states of delight, interest, and enthusiasm with being judged and rejected. Over the course of our time together, he began to unwind this organization and was able to slowly re-embody to this spectrum of experience and touch the natural joy he had disconnected from at an earlier time in his life.

TO FEEL ALIVE AGAIN

Developmentally speaking, for some of us the natural, raw, human experience of pleasure or enjoyment activated complexes in our parents—for example, maybe it triggered anxiety or discomfort in Mom and anger or impatience in Dad or caused others to shame or pull away from us. In our attempt to make sense of the rupture, we came to conclude *that joy was not okay*, destabilizing, and even potentially dangerous. But it was so natural to feel joy and to express that simple sense of aliveness, and it was baffling to discover that it led to our environment turning against us. As a little one, we were unable to understand what was going on and became confused as we began to associate the experience of joy with being unsafe. We had no choice other than to repress the joy and disconnect from our innocent, playful, spontaneous nature, which required that we disowned those feelings when they organically arose in our experience.

It can be helpful as part of our inquiry to ascertain what specific feeling states, forms of vulnerability, personality traits, and aspects of ourselves we have (usually unknowingly) come to associate with emotional hurt and a sense that we're not safe. Although it might be obvious how negative feelings and behaviors (e.g., anger, judgment, jealousy, fear) create difficulties in our lives, we must also be open to exploring the ways more positive material was also required to be repressed. And, as always, remember that this activity of repression was intelligent and adaptive in the moment because it prevented the devastating consequences of a wholesale withdrawal of affection, attention, and love from those around us.

As little ones with developing brains and nervous systems, we learn to disown or disavow *any* state of mind (and corresponding behavior) that has the potential to disrupt the tie to critical attachment figures. Although we can honor the adaptive and even lifesaving aspect of these defensive strategies, many of us long to know joy again, to feel alive, and to fully and spontaneously participate in our lives. Until we can provide a home for the entirety of who we are to live and breathe and have permission to be here in this world, we might always feel separate and disconnected from life. By learning to befriend ourselves in new ways, the central organizing theme of this book, we offer this field of permission for the lost pieces of soul to return, to share their essence and wisdom, and to walk with us as allies toward a new way.

To retrain ourselves to feel joy is not an easy path because by definition we will have to step back through anxiety and feelings of potential abandonment and overwhelm that the repression of joy (or whatever the relevant state is for us) has served to protect us from. It can be helpful to remember the possibility, as we've been exploring together, that although a part of us genuinely wishes to heal and live in a new way, other parts have an agenda of keeping us safe and protected, which can set up a contradictory state of affairs. Some part of us knows that if we heal from these earlier ways of organizing our experience, we will not be able to count on our previous strategies to protect us from a more naked, unguarded, and undefended relationship with life. On the one hand, this is what we've been longing for, to fully participate in an open, spontaneous, and free way, but on the other hand, we must honor the revolutionary implications of what true healing requires.

SHADOW, SYMBOL, AND DREAM

Sometimes people will go out of their way to explain to me how independent they are. They might talk about how through a lot of inner work, they've come to a place where they don't really need anyone, they can handle things on their own, and they've escaped from the messy territory of codependency.

Later in the conversation, perhaps, they'll share an encounter they had with a colleague at work who was so clingy, so dependent, and so sticky that it just made them feel angry, nauseous, claustrophobic, and so relieved they had somehow worked through all that. "Thank God that's not me anymore. God, they're annoying. I just don't understand how they can be like that. They should really take a look at themselves."

And then maybe the next week they'll bring in a dream in which they were out on a walk and came across an inconsolable little infant who wanted to be held, to feel the warmth of skin-to-skin contact, but the dreamer just got more and more anxious and ran into the forest. It just felt so desperate and off-putting.

That with which we are not able or willing to be in conscious relationship within ourselves will have no choice but to manifest outside us, in relatively innocent others just being themselves, in dream figures, in unexpected irrational moods, in fantasies, in symbols, in images, and even in the natural world as animal friends, sunrises, colors, and water.

These ones appear not as some cruel cosmic trick or joke or to attack, harm, or take us down but as orphaned pieces of soul, shards of psyche, slivers of heart cells longing to return home, take their place at the table of the vast, contribute, share, dance, play, and remind us of how rare and precious it is here.

Between the extremes of independence and dependence, selfishness and selflessness, meaning and meaninglessness, order and disorder, and oneness and multiplicity is a rich, majestic middle area filled with scintillas of light, strands of creativity, and aliveness of soul. To turn back toward the lost opposite is an expression of mercy and a manifestation of grace.

It is an act of love not only for ourselves but for others and for all of life, for earth and the ancestors, for the animals and streams and stars, and also for the ones circling now, awaiting fertile and ripe conditions for their arrival here.

THE OTHERNESS OF SHADOW

Emotionally sensitive, somatically grounded inner work is distinct for each nervous system. You must discover for yourself the most skillful, effective, and compassionate ways to open your body, psyche, and heart. No one can tell you what the right way is for you. The journey is individual by nature, requiring primary experience; collective spirituality might not be able to meet the longing within you. Although many mentors and guides appear as signposts along the way, the true teacher or teachings will always point you back into your own uniqueness by way of a secret language only you can decipher. The journey of the heart is radical and revolutionary and requires you, *exactly as you are*, in all your chaotic glory. In this sense, you *are* the *prima materia* without which the Great Work cannot proceed.

It is difficult to do shadow work on our own because by definition we cannot see it, at least not clearly. It is often best approached in connection with an attuned other, where we can make use of the energy and dynamics of the relational field to help us see in the dark, in "borrowing" another's soothed, calm nervous system as we enter uncharted territory and as we open ourselves to the inner figures and pieces of the soul that have become lost along the way. It is not easy to find these ones on our own because the landscape is hazy, the forests are misty and thick, and we all have within us a propensity to maintain life as it is. This "other" need not take expression within a professional relationship, such as with a therapist, coach, or counselor, though of course that is a valid pathway for some. Any person we trust who resonates with us, who can listen carefully and empathically with a limited agenda, and who shares an intention to bear witness and travel with us into the depths of our experience can be helpful.

I want to make it clear that although shadow work is often best undertaken with an "other," I am not saying it is not possible to engage it on our own. Much of the territory we cover together here in this book is supportive of recognizing, illuminating, and "reowning" the shadow, a sacred activity we do for ourselves as well as for others. As we become more acquainted and conversant with the inner territory of psyche, body, and heart, we can develop a more intimate and illumined relationship with the various "internal" others as they appear through our dreams as well as in the waking state in moments of meditation, inquiry, and contemplation, and as they emerge within our close personal relationships. We begin to see how we take unwanted qualities that are part of us and "locate" them in another object, person, or group of persons. And from this seeing, the path of "reclaiming" the shadow begins to make sense to us experientially; we start to "reown" that material and provide a home for it within ourselves.

The important point here is that the shadow has the sense of being "other" to us, that is, "other" to our ordinary standpoint of ego consciousness. At first glance, it doesn't seem to "fit in" so well, but there is something (hauntingly) familiar about it. To honor the otherness of the shadow, whether via another person, dream image, strange bodily sensation, intense emotional state, or other aspect of our experience with which we're not usually in touch that feels "foreign" is helpful in bringing the shadow out of the shadow so that we can work with it. Remember that the shadow is not evil or an enemy but a lost part of ourselves that seeks illumination so that it can resume its rightful place in the larger ecology of what we are.

The way of direct revelation and embodied, experiential discovery is not the easy way. It is not the path of five clear steps to empowerment, manifestation, or thinking our way into permanent happiness, abundance, and bliss. It is not about learning a bunch of new powerful techniques or the latest awakening technology. There is nothing wrong with these approaches per se, but mine is only an invitation to keep our eyes open and realize we might never be able to fully touch the mystery with technique or prefabricated steps and stages. We must discover the secret map within us, hidden inside our hearts, and cultivate the courage and the trust to follow our own path, at times to walk alone and at other times to make the journey side by side with a kindred traveler who can see into our shadow in ways we cannot see on our own. How this "kindred traveler" takes form is a mystery and often comes into our lives in surprising and unexpected ways.

THE THRESHOLD OF A NEW WORLD

From an alchemical perspective, wisdom hidden in the core of our so-called negative emotions is not available by privileging and attending only to "positive" states such as joy, happiness, clarity, and peace. If our relationship with the "material" of our lives is oriented around purging or even more subtly transforming or "healing" it (at least at first), we might never be able to get close or intimate enough to mine the intelligence concealed in its core. Although positive qualities and experiences are also of course valid, honorable, and worthy of cultivation and ongoing relationship, they do not represent the *entirety* of what it means to be a living, breathing, sensitive human being. If our emphasis is to eradicate the unwanted material from our systems as quickly as possible, we sacrifice powerful opportunities for self-awareness. This deeply rooted urge to rid ourselves of parts of the personality we have deemed "negative" reflects a larger cultural rejection of the darkness and the creative, yet misunderstood, unknown territory of the alchemical *nigredo*. When we are in an awake, embodied, and compassionate relationship with shadow elements and less-than-desired aspects of ourselves, we can work with and integrate them rather than project them onto others and into the world.

As we are able to provide holding and attunement for even our most undesirable qualities, we might come to the profound realization that none of this needs to be "let go" by way of some active, controlling process and procedure. Rather, it will organically "let go of us" when we meet it in open awareness, metabolize it, and find that its previous role and function are no longer required. The war is ended. When we allow the wisdom inherent in psychic experience to come through the symptom and for its messages to be decoded, we find ourselves at the threshold of a new world. When the energies and figures of the inner landscape have been acknowledged, tended to with care, and touched with curiosity and awareness, they soften and resume their rightful place in the overall ecology of being.

In the Dzogchen tradition of Tibetan Buddhism, it is said that the nature of all experience is to "self-liberate" when we meet it with open, warm, agendaless, naked awareness. I find this image of "self-liberation" rich, evocative, and helpful. In other words, painful thoughts and feelings do not require active effort on our part to transform, transmute, or reveal their primordial nature. We do not need to get rid of, shift, or even "heal" these difficult states or convert them into their opposites but only to infuse them with presence, bearing witness to how they arise, dance for a short while, and dissolve on their own in the context of an enormous amount of space. In this practice, we begin to discover they are not obstacles on our path but illumined lanterns in the darkness.

It can take some time and experience to allow this realization to filter in and wash through our bodies, nervous systems, and hearts. From this deeper layer of meeting them at a more energetic level, we discover that we need not do anything active in order to "transform" them but only hold and touch them with greater awareness, mercy, and compassion. And then whether they are coming, going, or staying becomes secondary, for we see that our suffering and struggle is not inherent in these feeling states but arises out of a shift in our *relationship* with whatever appears. This is a profoundly empowering realization. As with a house guest we recognize as a part of ourselves and a carrier of important guidance for our ongoing journey, even if at times they are disturbing or provoking, we allow them the space to come, to stay for a while, and eventually to move on. We care for them, nurture them, and are curious about them, while at the same time we establish healthy boundaries so that we do not fuse or become enmeshed or flooded by them. We meet them in this alchemical middle territory, which is intimate but always a bit uncertain and unknown, full of possibility, creative, and alive.

ANGER AND RAGE AS PORTAL

As I noted earlier, one of the more common experiences we either deny, repress, or act out in unhealthy ways is that of anger. Rather than cultivating a conscious, embodied, and curious relationship with this natural energy, we often engage in a variety of inner and outer behaviors to avoid meeting it directly. But no matter how hard we try, at times the visitor of rage will push its way into conscious awareness. We might envision it as an ancient companion from whom we had to split off at an earlier time, despite it being a valid and sane response to terror, abuse, neglect, and boundary violation . . . a natural reaction to narcissistic injury and a deeply misattuned world.

In just this one moment, receive and touch this anger. Be touched by it, for just one second, or two. Fully. Not partially. Speak with the angry one, listen to him, at a pace that is provocative, yet safe enough. Feel what he is feeling, see what she is seeing, imagine what they have come to imagine; be a vessel in which this one can find sanctuary and safe passage from an exhausting journey. Open a dialogue into relationship with this forgotten soul part who has returned, longing to be allowed back home.

We all know the tragic effects of disavowing our anger, denying this one a seat at the table of Being. But sending it into the underworld does not purge or heal him or her. Pretending we're never angry, discharging the feeling in unconscious behaviors, or engaging a fantasy that it's not "spiritual" to have feelings of rage only allows the emotion to gain energy like a psychic tornado, spinning and gathering force within the shadow, where it will eventually surge, often in ways that can be incredibly destructive.

Separate a bit from the anger so that you do not fuse with it. The invitation is to move close but not too close. Open to an intimacy without fusion, honoring your own integrity as you enter the interactional field. "I will enter relationship with you but will not merge with you. I am listening. I will no longer deny you, but I will not be flooded and taken over by you. I will meet you in the middle. We will work together now to protect and defend my own integrity but in a way that also honors my vulnerability, sensitivity, and eccentricity. I will no longer deny you, but I will not allow you to control me. I will consider your position, but I will have the ultimate say."

Find a provocative but not overwhelming boundary. In this liminal, in-between state, we don't repress, dissociate, or split, but we also do not fall in, drown, and act out in unhealthy, habitual, and addictive ways. In the alchemical middle, rage is not a toxin we must expunge from what we are but an intense and wrathful energy, an organic part of the human psyche that only longs to be integrated and provided its rightful home. Anger is life itself, wanting to be known and here to serve a vital function, but it must be understood, digested, touched, and metabolized in order for its intelligence to flow.

In this sense, anger is not something that needs to be fixed, cured, or even healed. It is not a sin, and its wave-like appearance is not evidence that you have failed, fallen short, are not "spiritual," or have descended into a pathological state. It is evidence that you are alive, that you have a human nervous system, and that you are in touch with sacred life energy, albeit an energy often misunderstood. The anger is not the problem but its repression, dissociation, and acting out in an unconscious, disembodied way that can be so devastating.

With the fire of curiosity, deep care, and the commitment to no longer abandon yourself—and with the ally of the breath as your guide—descend into your belly, touch your heart, open a portal to your throat. Find the anger lodged in your somatic being, hiding out and pleading for reunion, buried in the old stories and the unfelt emotions. Make a journey into the core of the rage and feel the feelings, sense the sensations, and touch the raw, shaky life longing to be held. Dare to see this one not as enemy but an ally and harbinger of integration.

By way of this journey, anger will be revealed as what it is, a secret wisdom-guide and bridge into the universal heart—a messenger of power, clarity, and fierce compassion that wants you as its midwife. In ways that seem contradictory and paradoxical, befriending this anger opens a portal into connection with others—others external to us as well as lost figures and pieces of soul within—so that we may live and move and dance with them in skillful, wise, sensitive, and compassionate ways.

PROJECTION AND THE MYSTERIOUS OTHER

It can be fascinating (and disturbing) to see how we locate and discover qualities in others with which we long to be in touch in ourselves but for one reason or another have turned from and disowned. It is no coincidence that we tend to attract and are attracted to (as well as repel and are repelled by) those we perceive as embodying a quality we've lost contact with internally. To return to a previous example, say we meet with someone we see as being extraordinarily dependent. They nag their partner, are super clingy and unable to function on their own, and manifest an overall repulsive state of neediness. We are nauseated. "God, what is wrong with them? They are clearly lost in some state of codependence. I feel sorry for them. They are so annoying. Grow up!" Moreover, we assure ourselves by noting there is no way we would ever be like that.

Of course, our observations could be "true" about the other, but for the purposes of this vignette, that is not the point. As Jung clarifies, projection rarely flows in one direction only; the recipient will often provide a "hook" upon which we can hang our projection.[1] In this sense, projection is an interpersonal process, occurring at the intersection of the conscious and unconscious aspects of two subjectivities, not just something one party is doing to another.[2] What we're on the lookout for is an irrational, emotional reaction on our part in response to the relatively innocent behavior of another. This reactivity can come about in a conversation with someone we know well or even in our observation of a stranger across the room with whom we have absolutely no history. Somehow, just by being themselves, the other triggers an unexplainable surge of feeling, rage, irritation, embarrassment, or fascination. What is happening here?

As I've mentioned, as young children we made the (usually unconscious) decision to disconnect from certain feelings and parts of ourselves that threatened to disrupt the tie with important caregivers. We are wired to do whatever possible to keep the connection intact, even if the resulting contact was misattuned, neglectful, or even (sadly) abusive. In the tender, developing nervous system of a little one, some contact is better than none. At times, maintaining connection required that we split off from native ways of being and disconnect from parts of ourselves, including even which ideas and emotional experience were permitted to be felt and expressed. As painful as this was, the capacity to disconnect in this way was an act of intelligence and creativity at the time, an early attempt at self-care, and it served a critical survival function.

Although I believe that on some deep level we have a genuine longing to reclaim these lost soul parts and unique expressions of our personalities, it can feel unsafe to allow them back in consciously and *directly*, for we sense that to do so might generate too much anxiety and uncertainty. If we re-embody to these orphaned aspects of our experience, how will others respond? Will they abandon us? Shame us? Meet us with rage, disappointment, and judgment? Will they withdraw affection, love, and holding as was the case in earlier times when we took the risk to be ourselves? Yes, on the one hand we yearn for reunion with the entirety of what we are, but on the other hand there is understandable concern that it just won't be safe to do so.

By locating (finding) these qualities in another, however, we can explore what we've disconnected from at a distance in a way that feels safer. There is a real intelligence in this we can honor; there's no need to shame or judge ourselves for "projecting" and not being able to immediately call forward the lost essences within. We all project, and by "all" I really do mean *all*; it is a natural function of the human psyche, not a fault to attack as evidence of our psychological or spiritual immaturity.

As we bring more awareness to what's going on during these unique moments of activation, we can begin to open to the possibility of reclaiming core parts of ourselves along with the associated emotional experience we had to disown at an earlier time. There is nothing wrong with turning to another to help us access and integrate aspects of ourselves with which we have lost contact; as always, the invitation is not to never do this but to bring as much consciousness and compassion as we can to what is happening. We can be sensitive to the burden we might be placing on another to care for our lost emotional world for us, which even if they love us profoundly, they cannot do. In fact, they might come to unconsciously (or otherwise) resent us for asking that they do this because they sense at a deep level that they will not ultimately succeed. They can help tremendously, of course, creating a sanctuary within the relational field where we might be able to feel safer (at times), contact more insight and self-awareness, and open where such opening was not previously possible.

Over time, yes, we can locate this activity inside and learn to provide that function and field of safety for ourselves. It's not a matter of *either or* but of *both and*, when at times we allow ourselves to reach out to another for help and at other times make effort to provide that attunement, holding, and care for ourselves. We can build these resources slowly, over time, generating deeper levels of trust in ourselves to wisely and compassionately tend to whatever inner state presents itself. With practice, we can internalize this environment of attunement and safely gather the pieces of psyche, soma, and soul.

FORERUNNERS OF INTEGRATION

Whenever you find yourself surprised at how triggered you become toward a certain person, thrown off center by some way they act or speak, annoyed or irritated beyond what seems appropriate for the situation— or even infatuated with them in a way that seems surprising—slow down and pay careful attention. Something important is being presented. An invitation is being offered. Be kind to yourself. Be curious. No shame, blame, or judgment. Just curiosity and kindness. Before you act, which can seem so urgent in the moment, just pause for a second and bring awareness to the overall situation. If you can, make a quick scan throughout the layers of experience—core beliefs, overall mood, felt sense in the body, impulses to *do* something.

Again, look for responses that are irrational, overblown, and seem to occur on their own, out of the blue, in a surge of unexpected feeling, and you become hooked into a cascade of thoughts, images, emotions, and sensations in the body. Jung speaks about the autonomous nature of this material, in which for a moment what he calls a "splinter personality" takes over ordinary ego consciousness and colors our perception, constellating powerful feelings and mental associations.[3] Usually, a lot of emotion is associated with our complexes, most provocatively activated in the context of relationship with others who, as we've been exploring, in one way or another carry qualities with which we have lost contact in ourselves. Anytime we're observing another or in dialogue with them and a flood of ruminating thoughts or cascading feelings comes into the field, it is an invitation for us to slow down and to get really curious: What's going on here?

It's important to note I'm *not* speaking about passively standing by, slowly working with your complexes or engaging *any* other inner work for that matter, if someone is being abusive or disrespectful to you, and they are unloading their unconscious onto you in a way that is aggressive or unsafe. In these situations, please confront the situation directly, enact a clear boundary, and *act* to stand up for yourself. What I'm addressing here are situations in which this *isn't* happening, and the other *isn't* doing anything *to* you but just being themselves, and seemingly out of nowhere you notice yourself in a totally reactionary state, flooded with feelings, images, and thoughts that seem excessive and as if they have come out of nowhere.

Although it's heartening to see pockets of greater interest in shadow work and projection in the greater culture, as with all subtle teachings, those on shadow can be co-opted to validate all sorts of unhealthy and narcissistic behavior. An example is acting in a way that is deeply unkind and unconscious, then in response to being called out on it, stating unequivocally and with an inflated spiritual ego, "Oh, *that's just your own projection.*" I'm sure you know what I mean. That is *not* what I'm describing here.

Rather, I'm addressing those relatively harmless, more neutral situations in which, before you know it, you're hooked into an unexpected surge of emotion, lashing out at the other, critiquing, judging, attacking them (or yourself) in a way that, on deeper reflection, just feels a bit overdone. Or maybe you're idolizing them, turning them into a savior, irrationally falling in love with them in a way that just doesn't fit with the actual situation on the ground. In these moments, material from the unconscious is attempting to make its way to the surface, not to harm or throw us off course but as a forerunner of integration.

AN EXPERIMENT IN ILLUMINATING PROJECTION

One way to explore this material for yourself is to ask: What qualities in others (positive or negative) have an uncanny ability to throw me off-center, triggering an avalanche of charged feelings, images, urges, and sensations? What gets my mind racing and feeling all hot and bothered, hooked and claustrophobic, or enraged and activated in a way that seems exaggerated? We can of course look out for this in a moment of actual interchange with another, which might be the most powerful (yet difficult) way to explore this material, but it can also be done as a meditation, by way of imagination and visualization.

For example, bring a person to mind who has a way of inducing these sorts of reactions within you—someone who triggers anger, annoyance, hatred, or aggression. Or, from the more positive side, maybe they excite you or you long to get closer and urgently move toward them, or in some way you idolize them or have placed them onto a pedestal. These reactions appear in ways that seem extravagant or otherwise not fully based in reality.

For just a moment, set aside any interpretation of what might be happening as well as any demand to understand or analyze what's going on.

Let the "external" person go and see if you can open to an "internal other" arising now to be known, held, and allowed back inside. Scan your body and the felt sense of the overall situation and atmosphere, and use your breath to stay close to yourself. Provide a home for the lost ones to return.

What has this person activated in you? What is most needing extra attention and loving awareness in this moment of activation? What has the "external" other come to remind you of? What quality or aspect of yourself have you fallen out of relationship with for which this one is opening a doorway into reunion?

As you contact this material within you, go slowly and bring as much curiosity as you are able to what is wanting to be met. Allow it to make itself known across the various layers of experience, including through thoughts, underlying beliefs, feelings, emotions, sensations, memories, images, and urges to act. Separate from it a bit so that you can maintain perspective but not so much that you lose close contact. Provide sanctuary for the material and the figures to dance and speak to you and tell you what they need and why they have come. Engage in active dialogue and inquiry for a while, and then rest. Allow the visualization to dissolve back into the open space from which it came.

ILLUMINATING NARCISSISTIC ORGANIZATION

As we explore the shadow and the role of the "other" in our lives and our capacity to attune as well as receive such attunement from them, it can be helpful to bring the topic of narcissism into our inquiry. The use of the word "narcissist" and the topic of narcissism is on the rise in contemporary culture and is employed in a variety of ways and contexts. Many different meanings are ascribed to the notion of narcissism and there is quite a lot of confusion about it. Narcissism unfolds along a spectrum, from what we might refer to as "healthy" or "functional" narcissism on one end of the scale (referring to a basic sense of self-worth, ego strength, and self-esteem) to pathological, destructive narcissistic personality disorder on the other. The great pain, trauma, neglect, and abuse as a result of narcissistic injury are incredibly important (and heartbreaking) topics, including how to best help our dear brothers and sisters who have fallen prey to the devastating effects of narcissistic behavior in all its forms. Let us each take a moment to send our blessings, thoughts, and love to all victims of narcissism, along with our prayers that they find their birthright of healing, peace, and the true joy.

Here, rather than addressing clinical, pathological narcissism (again, an important topic but outside the scope of this book), I want to share a few thoughts about the nature of narcissism more generally and how we can come to bring light to our *own* narcissistic tendencies. The intention in doing so is to cut off unhealthy narcissism at its root and to do everything we can to reduce its effects and impact in our world. In order to accomplish this, we must discover the seeds, roots, and branches of narcissism within ourselves and illuminate this material with new levels of awareness, compassion, and clear seeing, not to shame ourselves or others with what we discover but to untangle the unique web of dynamics that can be so devastating for the soul, with the intention that the intergenerational transmission of unhealthy narcissism be interrupted, depotentiated, and ultimately ended. I realize it might feel like a mighty task, but it is up to us to do this for our ancestors, and for those yet to come—for the little babies being born now, and for all life everywhere.

An indicator of narcissism is the inability to see the other as a *subject* in their own right. Instead, they are apprehended and related to as a mere *object* in our own awareness. It is that failure to hold the other as an *actual person* with their own ways of perceiving and making sense of their lives that lies at the root of narcissistic organization. When caught in the trance of narcissistic perception, we are unable to distinguish the other as having their own *interiority* and *subjectivity*, imbued with their own feelings, beliefs about themselves and the world, and unique ways of making meaning of their experience. We are unable to see them as a person with their own hopes, fears, values, longings, and dreams, which might or might not be similar to ours; in fact, they might be quite different or even contradictory. But despite these dissimilarities, just like us, they want to be happy, to be at peace, to be free, to love and be loved. Just like us.

In a narcissistic state, we are unable to attune to the subjectivity of the other. Instead, we perceive them through the lens of whether and how they can meet our needs and reflect back to us our own basic goodness, with which we've lost touch in ourselves. In narcissistic organization, we search for this most primordial sense of self-worth in the eyes, words, and behavior of another, acting in whatever ways we must to compensate for our devastating feelings of unworthiness. Others are valued not according to their own distinctive qualities and unique interior experience but by their willingness and capacity to make us feel better about ourselves and remedy a profound self-hatred within us. In this sense, the other exists merely to serve a function in our own self-absorbed house of cards, an essential coconspirator required to keep our fragile sense of self from crumbling and exposing the shamefulness at the core.

In a narcissistic trance, we lose touch with the holy reality of the other. We don't see the miracle in front of our eyes. "Oh my god, this is another human being, a unique expression of life, not just someone sent to earth to mirror back my greatness, to reflect and buffer my self-image, and to care for and liberate the haunting ghosts of my unlived life."

It takes a lot of discernment to navigate this territory, to see how each of us from time to time perceive in this way in our relationships with others. It can be crushing (yet illuminating) to become aware of the ways we hold others as objects in our awareness, forgetting they are subjects longing to find meaning in their lives, to make sense of their

experience, and to engage the mystery in their own way. It is not easy
work and requires that we turn back toward a lot of feelings and parts
of ourselves we have managed to stay away from over the years. Caring
for the narcissist within us is a profound act of love, for ourselves and
others, and will go a long way to healing the personal and collective
pain and trauma in our world.

ILLUMINATING INTERNAL NARCISSISM

It is tempting (and much easier and less anxiety provoking) to locate
narcissism *outside* ourselves, in another, and of course at times it is
important and honorable to confront and call out the behavior of a narcissist and to care for ourselves and others in fierce, direct, and powerful
ways. To enact forceful boundaries, say no loudly and clearly, assert our
needs, engage in conflict, defend ourselves and others, and to make use
of energies of aggression is needed. All of this is, of course, important.

But, again, the primary invitation here is to cultivate the curiosity,
courage, and compassion to meet the narcissistic one within us. The
invitation is to illuminate this one, to bathe him or her in the light
of awareness, and to finally enter into relationship with this figure to
whom, in some sense, we feel so close but in another has retreated
into the underworld. Narcissism is not only a personal matter but is
cultural and archetypal. Just like Narcissus becoming enamored at his
own reflection, we each have the potential to become self-absorbed at
the expense of the integrity and interiority of the other. The challenge
is to retrieve the narcissistic one from the dark soil and shadowy nether
regions of the psyche and out into conscious awareness so that he or
she is not running the show from behind the scenes, in ways that will
inevitably generate further suffering for ourselves and others.

Through turning toward this one, we can discover that the inner
narcissist is not actually an enemy attacking from the outside but an
unmet part of us, in some crazy way one of love's children, requesting

a moment of our presence, kindness, and care. He or she has been shamed, ridiculed, and exiled from the inner ecosystem for so long and will continue to appear in limitless forms until allowed back home. In unconscious configurations, this one can create a lot of difficulties in our ability to be present and intimate with others but when integrated consciously can be used as a bridge of connection. After some light is thrown into the shadow, the healthy qualities of positive self-esteem and self-worth provide important scaffolding through which we can more safely open to our vulnerability, take risks in relationship, and rest in not knowing. And as a result, we won't be in a constant inner battle with ourselves and others, scrambling to prop up a fragmented sense of self and looking to others to mirror back to us our essential worth.

The importance of illuminating the shadow is so that we can provide sanctuary and safe passage for the unwanted parts of ourselves, previously abandoned feelings, and the darker aspects of our experience. As a result, paradoxically we release the light to come into our lives and into the atmosphere around us. The inner work we do is never for ourselves alone but for all of life, including the natural world. Through coming to trust in the ultimate workability and sacredness of what we once considered obstacles on the path, we discover in an experiential and embodied way that the path is in fact everywhere, that we are being invited in each moment to be crafted as a vessel in which love can come here to this place and heal and awaken everything it encounters.

As we end here, let us allow the implications of all this to flow through us and filter down into this world as we dedicate the work we have done and will continue to do to the liberation of all life everywhere. May this great befriending pour through our bodies and hearts and out into the four directions.

May all beings be safe, happy, and free. May each discover the majesty of the alchemical silver and gold hidden within, buried in the earth, and scattered in the stars. And in this discovery may we devote our lives to helping all form to know its essence.

EPILOGUE

How Well Did I Love?

SOMETIMES WE PRETEND THERE REALLY is something more than love that matters. We look up into the starry sky and are just not sure about it all. We know that somehow it must be possible for life to give us more: more connection, more grace, more awakening, more intimacy, more healing, more joy, more lovers. We wonder if we've done something wrong: perhaps we've not prayed hard enough, or in the right way; meditated enough; healed enough; hurt enough; opened ourselves enough; forgave enough; grieved enough; let things go enough, accepted enough, surrendered enough.

And then in the next moment, somehow something is different. The veil parts and for one microsecond we see what love is doing. We're given this much grace, to see for just one moment. The curtain is pulled back and we are shown. Despite the problems, the pain, the confusion, and the burden of becoming, our breath is taken and our hearts dissolve into the realization that there is no healing and no awakening coming in the future. The wholeness we long for is only now, even if paradoxically it is realized only within the very shards of our brokenness.

For just a brief moment, we see into the entire display. It is illuminated from within by a light crafted of an unknown source. What it reveals is the always, already raging perfection of this most sacred and rare human experience. Everyone we meet, every kind word that we speak, every time we touch another with our hands and with our hearts, each time we are called to be the space for another to remember the raging truth of what they are—somehow it has all been set up and orchestrated by love itself.

We are overwhelmed and awed by such intelligence, by this sort of cosmic creativity. And we know that in any moment that could ever be—whether joyful or sad or content or blissful or vulnerable or scared or confused or anxious or depressed or overflowing with gratitude—we could never find any separation between ourselves and love, between ourselves and life.

And then we look back up into that same sky . . . though something seems a little different. It's more vivid, the display more magical, we can hear the hum of the sacred world churning out the stars and each and every cell of each and every human heart. We behold Venus, the moon, the comets, this precious milky way that we call our home . . . with nothing left other than an unwavering faith in love's perfection.

We are relational beings with open, sensitive, vulnerable hearts and mirror neurons and can offer one another so much. May we listen to one another and attune deeply to what our sisters and brothers are feeling and how they are making meaning of their experience.

May we not shame the story they are telling or the ways they have come to imagine themselves and the world but to hold it in a spacious, compassionate, merciful awareness. May we allow it to touch us as we embrace the unknown together.

And may we truly allow the other to matter, to remember what is most important, to be held by the oceans and the trees, to fall to the ground in awe as the sun yields so that the moon and the stars may make their offerings once again.

In the busyness of the inner and outer worlds, we can so easily forget the miracle that is unfolding here moment by moment. The rarity and preciousness of the whole thing, being broken and whole together, never quite knowing how love will shapeshift and take form, even during difficult times. It can take our breath away. If we will allow it.

In those moments when our heart breaks in response to this world, the temptation can be overwhelming to put it back together again. But if we will ask the heart if it wishes to be mended, it will take us into the mystery. "In trying to heal me you remain too far away," the heart pleads with us. "I want you all the way inside, to bear witness to my brokenness, to stay close as I ache, to hold me, and I will show you the way home. Please don't turn."

Behind the scenes, love is at work, the beloved spinning out worlds of experience, longing to know itself through form, finding illumined passage through us as vessels of light and dark. Each time we listen carefully to another, speak kind words that validate and affirm, provide safe passage for their emotional world to be held and to unfold, we offer the gift of a soothed nervous system whereby they downregulate and rest . . . together we break more, burn more, and somehow become more whole.

HOW WELL DID I LOVE?

It is so easy to take for granted that tomorrow will come, that another opportunity will be given to bear witness to a sunset, take a walk in the forest, listen in awe to the birds, or share a moment of connection with the one in front of us. But another part knows how fragile it truly is here, how tenuous, and the reality that this opening into life will not be here for much longer.

Before we realize it, we can so easily fall into the trance of postponement. The spell of tomorrow looms large in the personal and collective psyche.

At the end of this life—which is sure to come much sooner than we think—it is unlikely we'll be caught up in whether we accomplished all the tasks on our to-do lists, played it safe, healed all the wounds from our past, wrapped up our self-improvement project, or completed some mythical spiritual journey.

Inside these hearts there may be only one burning question: How well did I love?

There are soul-pieces and lost parts orbiting in and around us, the ghosts of our unlived lives; those aspects of ourselves that have not been allowed sanctuary and permission. To attend to that which remains unlived—to listen to its poetry and provide a holding field for its emergence—is a radical, revolutionary act of compassion.

One day we will no longer be able to look at, touch, or share a simple moment with those we love. When we turn to them, they will be gone. One moment will be our last to encounter the immensity of one more breath, experience awe at a color or a fragrance or the blooming of a violet, or to enter into union with the vastness of the sea.

It will be our last chance to see a universe in a drop of rain, to have a moment of communion with a friend, or to weep as the light yields to the night sky.

One last moment to have a thought, feel an emotion, fall in love, or listen to a piece of music. To know heartbreak, joy, sorrow, and peace—to behold the outrageous mystery of what it truly means to be a sensitive, alive, connected human being.

What if today is that last day? Or tomorrow? Or later this week?

Knowing that death will come, how will we respond to the sacred and brief appearance of life?

Perhaps our "life's purpose" has nothing to do with what job we will find, what new thing we will manifest or attract for ourselves, or what mythical healing or awakening journey we will "complete." Perhaps the purpose of our life *is to fully live*, finally, to touch each here and now moment with our presence and with the gift of our one, wild heart.

And to do whatever we can to help others, to hold them when they are hurting, to listen carefully to the ways they are attempting to make sense of a world that has gone a bit mad. To slow down, in awe, and bear witness to the erupting miracle of the other as it appears in front of us. Perhaps this is the most radical gift we can give, to offer ourselves as a true healing space in which love can come alive here.

ACKNOWLEDGMENTS

MY HEARTFELT GRATITUDE TO THE GREAT internal Other, who continues to appear in her infinite forms, guiding me into the depths and secret places and revealing to me even a glimmer of the mystery. A special thank you to my dear friends and family who have held and supported me during the writing of this book, most especially Noah Licata, Charles Licata, Nancy Licata, Krista Marleena, and Jeff Foster. I'd also like to thank my dear friend Mirabai Starr for writing such a merciful and holy foreword and for participating in this project of love with me. Finally, I'd like to thank my friends at Sounds True, especially Tami Simon, Jaime Schwalb, and my editor Gretel Hakanson for their care and commitment to the Great Work and to the unfolding of soul in the world.

NOTES

Introduction

1. Edinger, *Anatomy of the Psyche*.

2. Although scholars debate the first appearance of the term *prima materia*, I refer to the work of C. G. Jung and James Hillman, as well as two of Jung's students who took a particular interest in alchemy: Marie-Louise von Franz (*Alchemy* and *Alchemical Active Imagination*) and Edward Edinger (*Anatomy of the Psyche*).

3. Jung, *Alchemical Studies*.

4. Edinger, *Anatomy of the Psyche*.

Chapter 1. Reimagining What It Means to Heal

1. I'd like to acknowledge and thank Caroline Myss (personal communication, 1996 and 1997) and Bruce Tift (*Already Free*, 2011, and personal communication, 2014) for introducing me to this idea and helping me to explore these unconscious processes in myself and others.

2. Tift, *Already Free*.

3. I'd like to acknowledge and thank Bruce Tift for introducing me to a stage-sensitive view of working with and integrating difficult emotional material, which I have adapted in part (*Already Free*, 2011, and personal communication, 2014).

4. Hayes and Smith, *Get Out of Your Mind and into Your Life*, 30.

Chapter 2. Already Held

1. Winnicott, *The Family and Individual Development*.

2. Welwood, *Healing the Core Wound of the Heart*.

3. Welwood, *Healing the Core Wound of the Heart*.

4. Siegel, *The Mindful Therapist*.

5. Heller and LaPierre, *Healing Developmental Trauma*.

6. Siegel, *Mindsight*, 137.

7. Jung, *Memories, Dreams, Reflections*.

Chapter 3. Self-Compassion and Caring for Ourselves in a New Way

1. Jung, *The Structure and Dynamics of the Psyche*.

2. Jung, *The Structure and Dynamics of the Psyche* (italics in the original).

3. See the groundbreaking work of Stephen Porges (2011, 2017, 2018) on the polyvagal theory for a detailed exploration of the autonomic nervous system and the sympathetic and parasympathetic pathways available in a moment of activation.

Chapter 4. A Sacred Deflation

1. American psychologist James Hillman and colleagues developed archetypal psychology as a post-Jungian form of psychology and psychotherapy that incorporated some of Jung's core ideas (although critical of others) with outside influences including Greek mythology, the Romantic and Renaissance traditions, the Sufi imaginal approach of Henry Corbin, and the larger field of depth psychology, including the work of Sigmund Freud and Alfred Adler. For an introduction to the field, see Hillman, *Archetypal Psychology*, *Re-Visioning Psychology*, and *A Blue Fire* (Thomas Moore, ed.), as well as Moore (2005, 2016) for a more popularized and accessible rendering.

2. Trungpa, *Lion's Roar*, 161–75.

3. Stolorow, *Trauma and Human Existence*.

Chapter 5. Shifting Our Center of Gravity

1. Siegel, *Mindsight*, 64.

2. Hillman, *The Alchemy of Psychology*.

3. Jung, *Mysterium Coniunctionis* (italics mine).

4. Wallin, *Attachment in Psychotherapy*.

5. Hillman, *The Alchemy of Psychology*.

6. Hillman, *Alchemical Psychology*, 123.

7. Siegel, *Mindsight*; Jung, *Mysterium Coniunctionis*.

8. Wallin, *Attachment in Psychotherapy*.

Chapter 6. The Great Dance of Being and Becoming

1. This dialogue between consciousness and the unconscious resulting in the emergence of a new and more integrated "third" position is the essence of what Jung called "the transcendent function." The essay "The Transcendent Function" appears in *The Structure and Dynamics of the Psyche*.

2. For more on the multiplicity of the psyche and the implications of this for psychological healing and transformation, see Hillman, *Re-Visioning Psychology*; Schwartz, *Internal Family Systems Therapy*; Stone and Stone, *Embracing Ourselves*; and Earley, *Self-Therapy*.

3. Turning an emotion or other inner experience into a figure for dialogue, via the imaginative faculty of the psyche, is an important methodology within analytical and archetypal psychologies, as discussed, for example, in Jung, *Memories, Dreams, Reflections* and *The Red Book*; and Hillman, *Re-Visioning Psychology*.

Chapter 7. Toward an Embodied, Emotionally Sensitive Spirituality

1. Welwood, *Toward a Psychology of Awakening*.

2. Ken Wilber, personal communication, 2014.

3. Wilber, *Spectrum of Consciousness*.

Chapter 8. Dancing in the Shadows

1. Jung, *The Structure and Dynamics of the Psyche*.

2. For an analysis of projection from an intersubjective systems perspective, see Stolorow, Brandchaft, and Atwood, 33–34.

3. Jung, *The Structure and Dynamics of the Psyche*.

BIBLIOGRAPHY

Alexander, F. G., and T. M. French. *Psychoanalytic Therapy: Principles and Applications.* New York: Ronald, 1946.

Bowlby, John. *Loss: Sadness and Depression*, vol. 3. New York: Basic Books, 1982.

Brach, Tara. *Meditation and Psychotherapy: A Professional Training Course for Integrating Mindfulness into Clinical Practice* (audio recording). Boulder, CO: Sounds True, 2011.

————. *True Refuge: Finding Peace and Freedom in Your Own Awakened Heart.* New York: Bantam, 2016.

Brandchaft, Bernard, Shelley Doctors, and Dorienne Sorter. *Toward an Emancipatory Psychoanalysis: Brandchaft's Intersubjective Vision.* Abingdon, UK: Routledge, 2010.

Buber, Martin. *I and Thou.* New York: Touchstone, 1971.

Chödrön, Pema. *Getting Unstuck: Breaking Your Habitual Patterns and Encountering Naked Reality* (audio recording). Boulder, CO: Sounds True, 2005.

Dieckmann, Hans. *Complexes: Diagnosis and Therapy in Analytical Psychology.* Asheville, NC: Chiron, 1999.

Earley, Jay. *Self-Therapy: A Step-by-Step Guide to Creating Wholeness and Healing Your Inner Child Using IFS, A New Cutting-Edge Psychotherapy.* Larkspur, CA: Pattern System, 2012.

Edinger, Edward. *Anatomy of the Psyche: Alchemical Symbolism in Psychotherapy.* La Salle, IL: Open Court, 1991.

Fenner, Peter. *Radiant Mind: Awakening Unconditioned Awareness.* Boulder, CO: Sounds True, 2007.

Hanson, Rick. *Hardwiring Happiness: The New Brain Science of Contentment, Calm, and Confidence.* New York: Harmony, 2016.

Hayes, Stephen, and Spencer Smith. *Get Out of Your Mind and into Your Life: The New Acceptance and Commitment Therapy.* Oakland, CA: New Harbinger, 2005.

Heller, Laurence, and Aline LaPierre. *Healing Developmental Trauma: How Early Trauma Affects Self-Regulation, Self-Image, and the Capacity for Relationship.* Berkeley, CA: North Atlantic, 2012.

Hillman, James. *Alchemical Psychology: Uniform Edition of the Writing of James Hillman,* vol. 5. Washington, DC: Spring, 2009.

———. *The Alchemy of Psychology* (audio recording). BetterListen! 2017.

———. "Anima Mundi: The Return of the Soul to the World." *Spring Journal* (1982): 71–93.

———. *Archetypal Psychology: Uniform Edition of the Writing of James Hillman,* vol. 1. Washington, DC: Spring, 2013.

———. *A Blue Fire.* Edited by Thomas Moore. New York: HarperPerennial, 1997.

———. *Re-Visioning Psychology.* New York: Morrow, 1997.

Hollis, James. *Finding Meaning in the Second Half of Life: How to Finally, Really, Grow Up.* New York: Avery, 2006.

Horvath, Adam O., and Leslie S. Greenberg, eds. *The Working Alliance: Theory, Research, and Practice.* Hoboken, NJ: Wiley, 1994.

Jung, C. G. *Alchemical Studies: The Collected Works of C. G. Jung,* vol. 13. Translated by R. F. C. Hull. Princeton, NJ: Princeton University Press, 1983.

———. *Memories, Dreams, Reflections.* Edited by Aniela Jaffe. New York: Vintage, 1989.

———. *Mysterium Coniunctionis: The Collected Works of C. G. Jung,* vol. 14. Translated by R. F. C. Hull. Princeton, NJ: Princeton University Press, 1977.

———. *Psychology and Alchemy: The Collected Works of C.G. Jung,* vol. 12, 2nd ed. Translated by R. F. C. Hull. Princeton, NJ: Princeton University Press, 1980.

———. *The Red Book: Liber Novus.* Edited by Sonu Shamdasani. New York: Norton, 2009.

———. *The Structure and Dynamics of the Psyche: The Collected Works of C. G. Jung,* vol. 8. Translated by R. F. C. Hull. Princeton, NJ: Princeton University Press, 1970.

Miller, Jeffrey. *The Transcendent Function: Jung's Model of Psychological Growth Through Dialogue with the Unconscious.* Albany: State University of New York Press, 2004.

Moore, Thomas. *Care of the Soul, A Guide for Cultivating Depth and Sacredness in Everyday Life.* Twenty-fifth anniversary edition. New York: HarperPerennial, 2016.

———. *Dark Nights of the Soul: A Guide to Finding Your Way Through Life's Ordeals.* New York: Avery, 2005.

Ogden, T. H. "The Analytic Third: Working with Intersubjective Clinical Facts." *International Journal of Psychoanalysis* 75 (1994): 3–19.

Papadopoulos, Renos, ed. *Carl Gustav Jung: Critical Assessments*. Abingdon, UK: Routledge, 1992.

Porges, Stephen. *Clinical Applications of the Polyvagal Theory: The Emergence of Polyvagal-Informed Therapies*. New York: Norton, 2018.

———. *The Pocket Guide to the Polyvagal Theory: The Transformative Power of Feeling Safe*. New York: Norton, 2017.

———. *The Polyvagal Theory: Neurophysiological Foundations of Emotions, Attachment, Communication, and Self-Regulation*. New York: Norton, 2011.

Rilke, R. M. *Letters to a Young Poet*. Translated by M. D. H. Norton. New York: Norton, 1934.

Rumi, Jalal al-Din. *The Essential Rumi*. New expanded edition. Translated by Coleman Barks. San Francisco: HarperOne, 2004.

Schore, Allan. *Affect Dysregulation and Disorders of the Self*. New York: Norton, 2003a.

———. *Affect Regulation and the Repair of the Self*. New York: Norton, 2003b.

———. *The Science of the Art of Psychotherapy*. New York: Norton, 2012.

Schuman, Marjorie. *Mindfulness-Informed Relational Psychotherapy and Psychoanalysis: Inquiring Deeply*. Abingdon, UK: Routledge, 2016.

Schwartz, Richard. *Internal Family Systems Therapy*. New York: Guilford, 1997.

Schwartz-Salant, Nathan. *The Mystery of Human Relationship: Alchemy and the Transformation of the Self*. Abingdon, UK: Routledge, 1998.

Siegel, Daniel. *The Mindful Therapist: A Clinician's Guide to Mindsight and Neural Integration*. New York: Norton, 2010.

———. *Mindsight: The New Science of Personal Transformation*. New York: Bantam Books, 2011.

Stein, Murray. *Jung's Map of the Soul: An Introduction*. Chicago: Open Court, 1999.

Stolorow, Robert. *Trauma and Human Existence: Autobiographical, Psychoanalytic, and Philosophical Reflections*. Abingdon, UK: Routledge, 2007.

Stolorow, Robert, Bernard Brandchaft, and George Atwood. *Psychoanalytic Treatment: An Intersubjective Approach*. Abingdon, UK: Routledge, 2000.

Stone, Hal, and Sidra Stone. *Embracing Ourselves: The Voice Dialogue Manual*. Novato, CA: New World Library, 1998.

Tift, Bruce. *Already Free: Buddhism Meets Psychotherapy on the Path of Liberation* (audio recording). Boulder, CO: Sounds True, 2011.

———. *Already Free: Buddhism Meets Psychotherapy on the Path of Liberation*. Boulder, CO: Sounds True, 2015.

Trealeaven, David. *Trauma-Sensitive Mindfulness: Practices for Safe and Transformative Healing*. New York: Norton, 2018.

Trungpa, Chogyam. *Cutting Through Spiritual Materialism*. Boston: Shambhala, 2002a.

———. *The Lion's Roar: An Introduction to Tantra*. Boston: Shambhala, 2001.

———. *The Myth of Freedom and the Way of Meditation*. Boston: Shambhala, 2002b.

———. *Shambhala: The Sacred Path of the Warrior*. Boston: Shambhala, 2007.

von Franz, Marie-Louise. *Alchemical Active Imagination*. Revised edition. Boston: Shambhala, 1997.

———. *Alchemy: An Introduction to the Symbolism and the Psychology*. Toronto: Inner City, 2015.

Wallin, David. *Attachment in Psychotherapy*. New York: Guilford, 2015.

Welwood, John. *Healing the Core Wound of the Heart* (audio recording). Boulder, CO: Sounds True, 2012.

———. *Toward a Psychology of Awakening: Buddhism, Psychotherapy, and the Path of Personal and Spiritual Transformation*. Boston: Shambhala, 2002.

Wilber, Ken. *The Spectrum of Consciousness*. Wheaton, IL: Quest, 1993.

Wilson, Robert Anton. *Prometheus Rising*. Las Vegas, NV: New Falcon, 1997.

Winnicott, D. W. *The Family and Individual Development*. London, UK: Tavistock, 1965.

ABOUT THE AUTHOR

MATT LICATA, PHD, is an independent scholar, psychotherapist, and writer based in Boulder, Colorado, who has spent the past thirty years immersed in the study of both psychological and contemplative approaches to psychological healing and spiritual transformation. Matt is author of *The Path Is Everywhere: Uncovering the Jewels Hidden Within You* (Wandering Yogi Press, 2017) and editor of *A Healing Space* blog. He offers in-person retreats each year in the United States and Europe, as well as online courses and events. To learn more about Matt and his work, please visit mattlicataphd.com.

ABOUT SOUNDS TRUE

SOUNDS TRUE is a multimedia publisher whose mission is to inspire and support personal transformation and spiritual awakening. Founded in 1985 and located in Boulder, Colorado, we work with many of the leading spiritual teachers, thinkers, healers, and visionary artists of our time. We strive with every title to preserve the essential "living wisdom" of the author or artist. It is our goal to create products that not only provide information to a reader or listener but also embody the quality of a wisdom transmission.

For those seeking genuine transformation, Sounds True is your trusted partner. At SoundsTrue.com you will find a wealth of free resources to support your journey, including exclusive weekly audio interviews, free downloads, interactive learning tools, and other special savings on all our titles.

To learn more, please visit SoundsTrue.com/freegifts or call us toll-free at 800.333.9185.